The Application of the OECD Model
Tax Convention to Partnerships

The Application of the OECD Model Tax Convention to Partnerships

A Critical Analysis of the Report Prepared by the OECD Committee on Fiscal Affairs

by

Michael Lang

LINDE
VERLAG
WIEN

KLUWER LAW
INTERNATIONAL
THE HAGUE - LONDON - BOSTON

This book is a coproduction of Linde Verlag Wien and
Kluwer Law International, The Hague

ISBN 3-85122-989-4 (Linde)
ISBN 90-411-9791-5 (Kluwer)

A-1210 Wien, Scheydgasse 24, Tel.: 01 / 278 05 26

Kluwer Law International, P.O. Box 85889, 2508 CN The Hague, The Netherlands.

Preface

The application of tax treaties to partnerships raises serious problems. It was therefore very well received by both practitioners and academics when the OECD Committee on Fiscal Affairs' Working Party No 1 formed a Working Group to study these problems in detail. The Working Group met a number of times from 1993 to 1997 and prepared a report on this subject which was published recently. This Report and the conclusions drawn by the Committee are analysed hereunder.

The assistants at the Department of Austrian and International Tax Law at the University of Economics and Business Administration in Vienna provided tremendous support in publishing this book. I would like to express a special thank you to Hans-Joergen Aigner. I would also like to thank Alexandra Beisteiner, Gabriele Bergmann, Silvia Neunteufl and Elisabeth Rossek for their dedicated support. Above all, I would like to express my grateful thanks to Martina Pasqualin for her tireless efforts in polishing up my English.

Michael Lang

Contents

List of Abbreviations

Art	Article
AWD	Außenwirtschaftsdienst des Betriebsberaters (periodical, Germany)
BB	Betriebsberater (periodical, Germany)
BFH	Bundesfinanzhof (German Federal Fiscal Court)
BIFD	Bulletin for International Fiscal Documentation (periodical, Netherlands)
BMF	Bundesministerium für Finanzen (Federal Ministry of Finance)
BStBl	Deutsches Bundessteuerblatt (German Federal Tax Gazette)
BTR	British Tax Review (periodical)
CDFI	Cahiers de droit fiscal international
CFA	Committee on Fiscal Affairs
CFC	Controlled Foreign Company
DB	Der Betrieb (periodical, Germany)
DStJG	Deutsche Steuerjuristische Gesellschaft
DStR	Deutsches Steuerrecht (periodical, Germany)
DStZ	Deutsche Steuerzeitung (periodical, Germany)
DTC	Double Taxation Convention
EC	European Communities
ECJ	European Court of Justice
ed(s)	editor(s)
EEC	European Economic Community
e.g.	for example
ET	European Taxation (periodical)
et al	and others
EU	European Union
EuZW	Europäische Zeitschrift für Wirtschaftsrecht (periodical, Germany)
EWS	Europäisches Wirtschafts- und Steuerrecht (periodical, Germany)
FG	Finanzgericht (German Fiscal Court)
FJ	Finanzjournal (periodical, Austria)
FR	Finanzrundschau (periodical, Germany)
id	idem (the same)
IFA	International Fiscal Association
Intertax	International Taxation (periodical)
IStR	Internationales Steuerrecht (periodical, Germany)
IWB	Internationale Wirtschaftsbriefe (periodical, Germany)

JbFfSt	Jahrbuch der Fachanwälte für Steuerrecht (Tax Lawyers Annual, Germany)
JBl	Juristische Blätter (periodical, Austria)
MC	OECD Model Convention
MC Comm.	Commentary on MC
m.no.	marginal number
No.	Number
OECD	Organization for Economic Cooperation and Development
ÖStZ	Österreichische Steuerzeitung (periodical, Austria)
P	The partnership
para	paragraph
RdW	Österreichisches Recht der Wirtschaft (periodical, Austria)
RFH	Reichsfinanzhof (Fiscal Court of the German Reich 1919–1945)
RIW	Recht der Internationalen Wirtschaft (periodical, Germany)
RStBl	Reichssteuerblatt (Tax Gazette of the German Reich)
sec	section
secs	sections
seq	sequential
StB	Der Steuerberater (periodical, Germany)
StbJb	Steuerberaterjahrbuch (Tax Consultants Annual, Germany)
StBp	Die steuerliche Betriebsprüfung (periodical, Germany)
StuW	Steuer und Wirtschaft (periodical, Germany)
SWI	Steuer und Wirtschaft International (Tax and Business Review; periodical, Austria)
SWK	Steuer- und WirtschaftsKartei (periodical, Austria)
v	versus
VCLT	Vienna Convention on the Law of Treaties
VfGH	Verfassungsgerichtshof (Austrian Constitutional Court)
vol	volume
VwGH	Verwaltungsgerichtshof (Austrian Supreme Administrative Court)
ZaöRV	Zeitschrift für ausländisches öffentliches Recht und Völkerrecht (periodical, Germany)
ZfV	Zeitschrift für Verwaltung (periodical, Austria)

List of Symbols

Indicates that the State treats partnerships as transparent entities

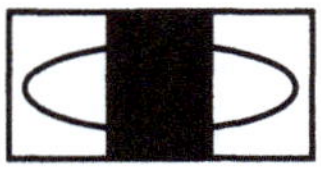

Indicates that the State treats partnerships as taxable entities

Indicates a partner of partnership P

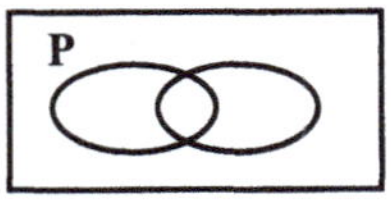

Indicates the partnership

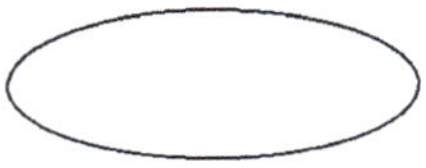

Indicates a fixed base or permanent establishment

Indicates a company

I. OECD Report on Partnerships

The application of tax treaties to partnerships raises serious problems. It was therefore very well received by both practitioners and academics when the OECD Committee on Fiscal Affairs' Working Party No 1 formed a Working Group to study these problems in detail. The Working Group met a number of times from 1993 to 1997 and prepared a Report on this subject which was published recently.[1] This Report and the conclusions drawn by the Committee are analysed hereunder.

The Committee adopted an approach based on the discussion of examples. This is a perfect way of focusing on practical problems. In dealing with these cases, the Committee tried to develop general principles. However an analysis of this Report has to summarize the principles that were developed by the Group and the underlying premises. Subsequently, this analysis tries to examine if the underlying premises are convincing and if the principles so developed were consequently followed.

[1] OECD, 'The Application of the OECD Model Tax Convention to Partnerships' in *Issues in International Taxation, No. 6* (1999).

II. Methodical Premises of the Report

1. The Relevance of the OECD Report and the Commentary to the OECD Model Tax Convention for the Interpretation of Tax Treaties

There are two reasons why it is important to clarify the legal relevance of the Commentary issued by the OECD Committee on Fiscal Affairs (CFA) before considering the conclusions drawn in the OECD Report. First, the OECD Report refers to the Commentary several times,[2] for the Drafters of the OECD Report the statements contained in the Commentary are important enough to be mentioned. Therefore, it has to be examined what relevance the Commentary has in the interpretation process. Secondly, the OECD Report proposes changes to the Commentary.[3] Therefore, it is important to know the effect which future changes of the Commentary might have for the interpretation of bilateral tax treaties.

The OECD CFA itself took a position on the issue and inserted the following statement in the introduction to the Commentary[4]: 'Needless to say, amendments to the Articles of the Model Convention and changes to the Commentary that are a direct result of these amendments are not relevant to the interpretation or application of previously concluded Conventions where the provisions of those Conventions are different in substance from the amended Articles. However, other changes or additions to the Commentary are normally applicable to the interpretation and application of Conventions concluded before their adoption, because they reflect the consensus of the OECD Member Countries as to the proper interpretation of existing provisions and their application to specific situations'.

The Committee proposes changes to the Commentary, and to a certain extent even to the OECD Model Tax Convention itself. But primarily the second part of the above-mentioned statement is of importance. The CFA is of the opinion that its Commentary is of relevance not only for the interpretation of future tax treaties, but also for those previously concluded. However, the CFA does not give any reasoning why it takes that position. The mere fact that the CFA takes this position is not enough, the CFA is not a law-making authority. It cannot decide on the relevance of its own statements. Therefore, one can just follow the position taken by the OECD if there is convincing reasoning behind it.[5]

---

2 OECD, supra note 1, at paras 24, 29, 33.

3 OECD, supra note 1, at paras 30, 32, 35, 56, 128.

4 OECD, *MC Commentary*, Introduction supra m.no. 35.

5 M. Lang, 'Die Bedeutung des Musterabkommens und des Kommentars des OECD-Steuerausschusses für die Auslegung von Doppelbesteuerungsabkommen' in Gassner, M. Lang and Lechner (eds), *Aktuelle Entwicklungen im internationalen Steuerrecht* (1994) (hereafter '*Entwicklungen*') p. 11 (p 20).

As tax treaties are part of public international law, their interpretation is governed by the Vienna Convention on the Law of Treaties (VCLT). According to Article 31 paragraph 1 of the VCLT, a treaty shall be interpreted in good faith in accordance with the ordinary meaning to be given to terms of the treaty in their context and in the light of its object and purpose. According to Article 31 paragraph 2 of the VCLT: 'the context for the purpose of the interpretation of a treaty shall comprise, in addition to the text, including its preamble and annexes:

a) any agreement relating to the treaty which was made between all the parties in connection with the conclusion of the treaty;
b) any instrument which was made by one or more parties in connection with the conclusion of the treaty and accepted by the other parties as an instrument related to the treaty'.

It is completely clear that changes and amendments to the Commentary are not made 'in connexion with the conclusion' of a treaty which was previously concluded. Therefore, a version of the Commentary drafted after a specific bilateral tax treaty that had already been concluded cannot qualify as part of the 'context' mentioned in Article 31 paragraph 2 of the VCLT.[6]

According to Article 31 paragraph 4, 'a special meaning shall be given to a term if it is established that the parties so intended'. This provision does not provide any legal basis to take into account a version of the Commentary drafted after a bilateral tax treaty has been concluded. A later version of the Commentary cannot offer any clues as to what had been the parties' intention at the time they negotiated the specific bilateral tax treaty.[7]

Another question is whether a new version of the Commentary could qualify as 'supplementary means of interpretation', mentioned in Article 32 of the VCLT. First of all, recourse may only be made to the supplementary means of interpretation to determine the meaning of a treaty provision 'when the interpretation according to Article 31

a) leaves the meaning ambiguous or obscure; or
b) leads to a result which is manifestly absurd or unreasonable'.

---

[6] Ault, 'The Role of the OECD Commentaries in the Interpretation of Tax Treaties' in Alpert and van Raad (eds), *Essays on International Taxation* (1993) (hereafter '*Essays*') p. 61 (p. 63); Avery Jones et al, 'The Interpretation of Tax Treaties with Particular Reference to Article 3(2) of the OECD Model' (1984) *BTR*, p. 14 and p. 90 (p. 92); M. Lang, in Gassner, M. Lang and Lechner (eds), *Entwicklungen*, pp. 16 et seq.; M. Lang, 'Haben die Änderungen der OECD-Kommentare für die Auslegung älterer DBA Bedeutung?' (1995) *SWI*, p. 412 (pp. 413 et seq.); Prokisch, 'Fragen der Auslegung von Doppelbesteuerungsabkommen' (1994) *SWI*, p. 52 (p. 53).

[7] Avery Jones et al, 'Article 3(2) of the OECD Model Tax Convention and the Commentary to It: Treaty Interpretation' (1993) *ET*, p. 252 (p. 255); M. Lang, in Gassner, M. Lang and Lechner (eds), *Entwicklungen*, p. 24; M. Lang, (1995) *SWI*, p. 413.

This leads to the result that the supplementary means of interpretation may be taken into account only in very rare situations. Secondly, as an example for the supplementary means of interpretation, the 'preparatory work of the treaty and the circumstances of its conclusions' are explicitly mentioned in Article 32 VCLT. Therefore, material may be taken into account which indicates the intention of the parties upon conclusion of a treaty. Again, the new version of the Commentary cannot be of relevance.[8]

However, under certain circumstances, the VCLT attributes special significance to any 'subsequent agreement' or 'subsequent practice' set out in Article 31 paragraph 3 of the VCLT. But the decision of the OECD CFA to amend or change the Commentary cannot qualify as an 'agreement' within the meaning of Article 31 paragraph 3 subparagraph (a) of the VCLT. This can be established by the fact that there is only a limited number of States which delegate representatives to the CFA which includes only OECD Member States.[9] And even if such treaties have been concluded between OECD Member States, neither the OECD Model Tax Convention nor the Commentary will qualify as an 'agreement' set out in Article 31 paragraph 3 subparagraph (a) of the VCLT. As such, the OECD Model Tax Convention and the Commentary do not constitute an international agreement, but were simply drafted by an international organization.[10] Even if the decision of an international organization could be—as Klaus Vogel suggests[11]—subsumed under the notion 'agreement' and at the same time one assumes that some kind of 'soft form' of an obligation can derive from a decision of the CFA, such a 'soft obligation' can only be addressed to the OECD Member States to follow the OECD Model Tax Convention in future treaty practice.[12] Conversely, a recommendation issued by OECD does not contain an obligation to construe in a different way existing tax treaties to which an unambiguous content can be attributed.[13]

The Commentary issued by the OECD CFA can equally not be seen as 'subsequent practice' as Article 31 paragraph 3 subparagraph (b) of the VCLT specifies. Referring to 'subsequent practice' does not cover every change of

---

[8] Ault, 'The Role of the OECD Commentaries in the Interpretation of Tax Treaties' (1994) *Intertax*, p. 144 (p. 148); M. Lang, in Gassner, M. Lang and Lechner (eds), *Entwicklungen*, pp. 28 et seq.

[9] Avery Jones et al, (1993) *ET*, pp. 255 et seq.; M. Lang, in Gassner, M. Lang and Lechner (eds), *Entwicklungen*, pp. 25 et seq.; M. Lang, (1995) *SWI*, pp. 413 et seq.; Vogel, *Double Taxation Conventions* (1997) Introduction supra m.no. 82 b.

[10] Avery Jones et al, (1993) *ET*, pp. 255 et seq.; M. Lang, in Gassner, M. Lang and Lechner (eds), *Entwicklungen*, pp. 25 et seq.; M. Lang, (1995) *SWI*, p. 414; Vogel, *Double Taxation Conventions* (1997) Introduction supra m.no. 82 b.

[11] Vogel, *Double Taxation Conventions* (1997) Introduction supra m.no. 80.

[12] M. Lang, in Gassner, M. Lang and Lechner (eds), *Entwicklungen*, pp. 25 et seq.; Vogel, *Double Taxation Conventions* (1997) Introduction supra m.no. 81 et seq.

[13] Ault, in Alpert and van Raad (eds), *Essays* (1993) p. 64.

an established treaty interpretation. A distinction has to be made between treaty interpretation as set out in Article 31 paragraph 3 subparagraph (b) of the VCLT and treaty amendments.[14] Article 31 paragraph 3 subparagraph (b) of the VCLT does not justify a change of an existing treaty provision. For that reason, the competence of tax authorities to establish a new interpretation of a certain treaty provision by starting a new 'practice' is restricted.[15] In addition, when applying the interpretation rules laid down in Article 31 VCLT, one has to distinguish between the different types of international treaties.[16] Since in many countries, tax law provisions require a clear wording so that every taxpayer knows in advance what his rights and obligations are, tax treaties should be considered part of those international treaties, where Article 31 paragraph 3 subparagraph (b) of the VCLT should be of only limited relevance.[17] 'Subsequent practice' should only be of relevance if—after using all means of interpretation—two alternative solutions are still available and neither of these solutions has a more convincing argument than the other.[18] This will happen only rarely, as taking into account not only the wording of a provision, but also the object and purpose and material produced in connection with the conclusion of the treaty, in many cases helps establish a convincing interpretation of a certain treaty provision. Therefore, a mere concurrent administrative practice adopted in both Contracting States cannot amend the treaty as such, even if it is supported by a new version of the Commentary.[19] Moreover, resorting to a new version of the Commentary not existing at the time the bilateral treaty was concluded, would also be contradictory to constitutional provisions in many countries.[20] Taking into

---

[14] M. Lang, in Gassner, M. Lang and Lechner (eds), *Entwicklungen*, p. 27; Ress, 'Die Bedeutung der nachfolgenden Praxis für die Vertragsinterpretation nach der Wiener Vertragsrechtskonvention' in Bieber and Ress (eds), *Die Dynamik des Europäischen Gemeinschaftsrechts* (1987) 49 (62).

[15] Bernhardt, 'Interpretation and Implied (Tacit) Modification of Treaties' (1967) *ZaöRV*, p. 491 (p. 496); M. Lang, *Doppelbesteuerungsabkommen und innerstaatliches Recht* (1992) (hereafter '*Doppelbesteuerungsabkommen*') p. 89; Verdross and Simma, *Universelles Völkerrecht* (1984) 506.

[16] M. Lang, *Doppelbesteuerungsabkommen* (1992) p. 90; M. Lang, in Gassner, M. Lang and Lechner (eds), *Entwicklungen*, p. 28; Ress, 'Wechselwirkungen zwischen Völkerrecht und Verfassung bei der Auslegung völkerrechtlicher Verträge' in *Berichte der Deutschen Gesellschaft für Völkerrecht*, Heft 23 (1982) p. 7 (pp. 13 et seq.); similar Klein, *Statusverträge im Völkerrecht* (1980) pp. 330 et seq.

[17] M. Lang, *Doppelbesteuerungsabkommen*, p. 90; M. Lang, in Gassner, M. Lang and Lechner (eds), *Entwicklungen*, p. 28.

[18] M. Lang, in Gassner, M. Lang and Lechner (eds), *Entwicklungen*, pp. 29 et seq.

[19] Karl, 'Sonstige Quellen des Völkerrechts' in Neuhold, Hummer, and Schreuer (eds), *Handbuch des Völkerrechts* (1997) 106 (109); M. Lang, in Gassner, M. Lang and Lechner (eds), *Entwicklungen*, pp. 31 et seq.

[20] M. Lang, in Gassner, M. Lang and Lechner (eds), *Entwicklungen*, p. 26; Vogel, *Double Taxation Conventions* (1997) Introduction supra m.no. 82 b; Wassermeyer, 'Diskussion' in Mössner and Blumenwitz (eds), *Doppelbesteuerungsabkommen und nationales Recht* (1995) pp. 85 et seq.

account a new version of the Commentary would mean that the OECD CFA would have the power to amend or change a bilateral tax treaty approved by the law-making body. Without further approval of the law-making body, a bilateral tax treaty could change its contents. In countries where international treaties rank equally with domestic statutes the aforementioned consequence would not be acceptable since the OECD CFA would have powers usually restricted to the law-making body.[21] The same concerns must be raised in view of the fact that the law-making process is governed in many countries by the separation of powers principle: the OECD CFA consists only of government representatives. If the OECD CFA would have the competence to influence the meaning of provisions of previously concluded tax treaties, the tax administration, acting jointly with those of other OECD member countries, would then have it completely in its power to amend the contents of the tax treaty without any determination.[22] Since such a practice would be contradictory to constitutional provisions in many countries, it is essential that attention should not be paid to Article 31 paragraph 3 subparagraph (b) of the VCLT as far as tax treaties are concerned. It cannot be assumed that tax treaty negotiators implicitly intended to refer to future changes and amendments of the Commentary if this would lead to questionable results from a constitutional point of view in many countries.[23]

What does this mean for the reasonings contained, and the conclusions drawn, in the OECD Report? As far as the OECD Report refers to statements mentioned in the Commentary, these references have to be examined very thoroughly. If such statements had not been part of the original version of the Commentary, dating from 1963, they can only be taken into account for the interpretation of bilateral tax treaties concluded after the publication of the version of the Commentary in which the referred statements were inserted.[24]

Another result of these deliberations is that changes and amendments to the Commentary proposed in the OECD Report may only be taken into account

---

[21] Barfuß, 'Rechtsstaat und völkerrechtlicher Vertrag' in Mayer et al (eds), *Staatsrecht in Theorie und Praxis, Festschrift Robert Walter* (1991) p. 25 (pp. 25 et seq.) (hereafter '*Staatsrecht*'); M. Lang, *Doppelbesteuerungsabkommen*, p. 87; M. Lang, in Gassner, M. Lang and Lechner (eds), *Entwicklungen*, pp. 26 et seq.; Thaler, 'Enthält das Wiener Übereinkommen über das Recht der Verträge verfassungsändernde Bestimmungen' in Mayer et al (eds), *Staatsrecht* (1991) p. 683 (pp. 693 et seq.).

[22] Wassermeyer, 'Diskussion' in Mössner and Blumenwitz (eds), *Doppelbesteuerungsabkommen und nationales Recht* (1995) pp. 85 et seq.; M. Lang, (1995) *SWI*, p. 414.

[23] M. Lang, 'Diskussion' in Mössner and Blumenwitz (eds), *Doppelbesteuerungsabkommen und nationales Recht* (1995) p. 87; Vogel, *Double Taxation Conventions* (1997) Introduction supra m.no. 82 b; Wassermeyer, in Mössner and Blumenwitz (eds,) *Doppelbesteuerungsabkommen und nationales Recht* (1995) pp. 85 et seq.

[24] M. Lang, in Gassner, M. Lang and Lechner (eds), *Entwicklungen*, pp. 13 et seq,; Vogel, *Double Taxation Conventions* (1997) Introduction supra m.no. 82 a; Wassermeyer, in Debatin and Wassermeyer (eds), *Doppelbesteuerung*, Vor Art. 1 supra m.no. 60.

for the interpretation of tax treaties concluded after the publication of the new version of the Commentary.[25] That does not necessarily mean that the OECD Report is completely meaningless for the interpretation of tax treaties previously concluded. The OECD Report is of importance insofar as its reasonings are convincing. The OECD Report is therefore as important as court decisions and scholarly writing. Its considerations will influence the interpretation of already existing tax treaty provisions in as far as they are convincing. To the extent the OECD Report just mentions that the Committee or its majority takes a certain position without giving the reasonings behind it, the OECD Report will not be of very great value in the interpretation process. Nevertheless, even such statements are of practical importance because they give an indication of the position that the tax authorities might take in a certain situation. This helps the taxpayer prepare his arguments to challenge his position in court if he does not find it appropriate.

On the other hand, it is clear that the OECD Report uses a valid argument if it refers to a version of the Commentary which was already publicly known at the time a certain bilateral tax treaty was concluded. The same is true for the interpretation of tax treaties being concluded after future changes and after the amendments of the Commentary are published. In this case, there is a valid assumption that tax treaty negotiators had the then-existing version of the Commentary in mind when they negotiated the provisions of a bilateral tax treaty. Where they followed the OECD Model Tax Convention, one might conclude that they wanted to create a provision having the same meaning which the Commentary gives to the corresponding provisions of the OECD Model Tax Convention. It is clear that the Commentary is part of the material which can be taken into account when interpreting the provision of the bilateral tax treaty.[26]

2. The Relation between Domestic Law and Tax Treaty Law

The purpose of the OECD Report on partnerships is not to clarify the relation between domestic law and tax treaty law. Nevertheless, an examination of the tax treaty treatment of partnerships is necessary to uncover the position one takes on the relation between domestic law and tax treaty law. Even if a writer avoids making an explicit statement on that topic, he implicitly takes a certain position. Therefore, it is necessary to know the position of the Committee on the relation between domestic law and tax treaty law.

The OECD Report does not contain a general statement on that issue. Nevertheless, the relation between domestic law and tax treaty law is mentioned

[25] See VwGH 31.7.1996, 92/13/0172.

[26] Ault, (1994) *Intertax*, p. 144; Avery Jones et al, (1993) *ET*, p. 255; M. Lang, in Gassner, M. Lang and Lechner (eds), *Entwicklungen*, p. 40.

several times:[27] in Section 62 of the Report, the Committee explains why it thinks that a certain approach is not 'inconsistent with the provisions of paragraph 2 of Article 3, under which terms not defined in the Convention have, unless the context provides otherwise, the meaning which they have under the domestic law of the Contracting State that applies the Convention. ... The Committee concluded that, in any event, if an interpretation based on domestic law would lead to cases where the income taxed in the hands of the residents of one State would not get the benefits of the Convention, a result that would be contrary to the object and purpose of the Convention, the context would require a different interpretation'.[28] This statement leaves the impression that the context—mentioned in Article 3 paragraph 2 of the OECD Model Tax Convention—requires an interpretation that entitles a resident of one Contracting State to the treaty benefits.

Although there are no general deliberations on that issue included in the OECD Report, in reading the Report one gets the impression that the Committee tends to understand provisions of the OECD Model Tax Convention by making reference to similarly worded provisions of the domestic law of the Contracting State applying the treaty. Making use of the 'context' seems to be the exception. The Report does not contain a convincing concept under which conditions preference is given to an interpretation deriving from the 'context' of the treaty. When the drafters of the OECD Report prefer not to refer to domestic law only single situations are mentioned.

The Committee even suggests a solution for 'qualification conflicts', 'due to differences in the domestic law between the State of source and the State of residence'[29]. The meaning of the phrase 'in accordance with the provisions of this Convention, may be taxed', contained in Article 23 OECD Model Tax Convention, is therefore being 'clarified' in that respect: 'Where, due to differences in the domestic law between the State of source and the State of residence, the former applies, with respect to a particular item of income, provisions of the Convention that are different from those that the State of residence would have applied to the same item of income, the income is still being taxed in accordance with the provisions of the Convention, in this case as interpreted by the State of source. In such a case, therefore, Article 23 requires that relief from double taxation be granted by the State of residence notwithstanding the conflict of qualification resulting from these differences in domestic law'.[30] The OECD Report makes a suggestion for the solution of a problem which arises only if one interprets Article 3 paragraph 2 of the OECD Model Tax Convention to mean that primarily reference should be

[27] OECD, supra note 1, paras 62, 97, 105, 121.
[28] OECD, supra note 1, para 62.
[29] OECD, supra note 1, para 105.
[30] OECD, supra note 1, para 105.

made to domestic law and looking at the 'context' of the tax treaty is the mere exception. This leads to the question whether there is need for such an interpretation of Article 23 OECD Model Tax Convention. Looking primarily at the 'context' of the tax treaty would minimize the need for an interpretation that repeatedly refers to the domestic law of one of the Contracting States. As the OECD Report does not deal with the interpretation of Article 3 paragraph 2 of the OECD Model Tax Convention, it should be considered whether the assumption made by the Report is correct.

Article 3 paragraph 2 of the OECD Model Tax Convention has, in its latest version, the following wording: 'As regards the application of the Convention at any time by a Contracting State, any term not defined therein shall, unless the context otherwise requires, have the meaning that it has at that time under the law of that State for the purposes of the taxes to which the Convention applies, any meaning under the applicable tax laws of that State prevailing over a meaning given to the term under other laws of that State'.

The meaning of this provision decisively depends on the meaning of the phrase 'unless the context otherwise requires'. The object and purpose of the Model Convention make it reasonable to assume that much weight should be given to that phrase.[31] Where situations in which reference to domestic law is made, and these occur often, double taxation and non-taxation would be the consequence. The meaning of terms used in tax treaty provisions given by domestic law can differ considerably.[32] If the Contracting States understood a certain term used in a tax treaty provision in the same way as this term is understood in the context of its domestic tax law, a common understanding of this tax treaty provision in both Contracting States would be endangered. An interpretation paying attention to the object and purpose of a tax treaty is therefore not in accordance with a practice-making repeated reference to domestic law.[33]

If the suggestion made by John F. Avery Jones was followed it would not change this conclusion. According to John F. Avery Jones a treaty is only

---

31 Gröhs and Herbst, 'Die Interpretation von Doppelbesteuerungsabkommen als Problem der Auslegung von völkerrechtlichen Verträgen im nationalen Recht' (1986) *ZfV*, p. 16 (pp. 23 et seq.); Gloria, 'Die Doppelbesteuerungsabkommen der Bundesrepublik und die Bedeutung der Lex-Fori-Klausel für ihre Auslegung' (1986) *RIW*, p. 970 (pp. 970 et seq.); M. Lang, *Hybride Finanzierungen im Internationalen Steuerrecht* (1991) p. 25 (hereafter '*Finanzierungen*').

32 Debatin, 'System und Auslegung der Doppelbesteuerungsabkommen' (1995) *DB* Beilage 23, p. 3; M. Lang, *Doppelbesteuerungsabkommen*, p. 109.

33 Bleckmann, *Grundprobleme und Methoden des Völkerrechts* (1982) p. 89 (hereafter '*Grundprobleme*'); M. Lang, *Finanzierungen*, p. 25; M. Lang, in Gassner, M. Lang and Lechner (eds), *Entwicklungen*, p. 36; M. Lang, 'Die Bedeutung des originär innerstaatlichen Rechts bei der Auslegung und Anwendung von Doppelbesteuerungsabkommen' (1999) *SWI*, p. 61 (p. 62).

'applied' when it limits a Contracting State in its application of its domestic law. A Contracting State that is not restricted in its taxing rights by a tax treaty does not 'apply' the tax treaty.[34] According to this suggestion, the number of cases in which both Contracting States 'apply' the same tax treaty provision is limited. However, that does not mean that such situations cannot occur. If for example, a tax treaty provides for a reduction of a withholding tax in one Contracting State and a tax credit of the remaining withholding tax in the other Contracting State, both Contracting States 'apply' the tax treaty in the way defined by John F. Avery Jones.[35] If they were allowed to make reference to their definitions of domestic law when interpreting the relevant tax treaty, a different interpretation of the same treaty provision in both Contracting States could be the consequence. Even if one focuses on the situation in which the application of a tax treaty provision leads just to the restriction of the taxing rights of one Contracting State, the question arises as to how a tax treaty provision is interpreted in the Contracting State which—according to the terminology used by John F. Avery Jones—does not 'apply' the tax treaty.[36] If one does not follow the additional suggestion made by John F. Avery Jones et al[37] and by the Committee[38] that the qualification of the source State is legally binding for the State of residence, which will be discussed later, the Contracting State which does not 'apply' the tax treaty provision—as interpreted by John F. Avery Jones—has no other alternative than to adhere to the interpretation deriving from the context. This means that the same treaty provision is again understood differently: according to the domestic law in the State of 'application', according to the result deriving from the 'context' in the other State.[39] Summing up, it is clear that John F. Avery Jones' suggestion to understand the phrase 'to apply' in another way as discussed above does not solve the problem created by an interpretation of Article 3 paragraph 2 of the OECD Model Tax Convention, which understands the phrase 'unless the context otherwise requires' as the exception to the general rule referring to domestic law causes.

Therefore bearing in mind that paying attention to the object and purpose of the OECD Model Tax Convention suggests putting considerable weight on the above-mentioned phrase 'unless the context otherwise requires', it makes sense to examine the wording in detail. The term 'context' may have a very broad meaning. It can cover not only the whole OECD Model Tax Convention but also the preparatory work of the OECD Model Tax Convention such

---

34 Avery Jones et al, (1984) *BTR*, p. 50; Avery Jones et al, (1993) *ET*, pp. 253 et seq.

35 Avery Jones et al, 'Credit and Exemption under Tax Treaties in Cases of Differing Income Characterization' (1996) *ET*, p. 118 (p. 120).

36 Avery Jones et al, (1984) *BTR*, p. 50.

37 Avery Jones et al, (1996) *ET*, p. 135.

38 OECD, supra note 1, para 102 et seq.

39 Avery Jones et al, (1996) *ET*, p. 135.

as the Commentary.[40] All historical, systematical and teleological aspects, which are important for the interpretation of the OECD Model Tax Convention may be taken into account.[41] If one applies such a broad understanding of the term 'context' it is hard to imagine finding a tax treaty provision whose meaning cannot be developed by thoroughly examining its 'context'. One is confronted with a similar challenge when one interprets domestic provisions. If for example a domestic tax law provision does not make reference to other parts of domestic law, one has no choice than to look for all historical, systematical and teleological aspects of this provision and try to establish its meaning. Usually, this will be successful. There is no reason why one should not successfully establish the meaning of a provision from its context just because the provision is not of domestic but of international origin.

According to the wording of Article 3 paragraph 2 of the OECD Model Tax Convention the 'context' has to 'require' its relevance, otherwise recourse is made to domestic law. Klaus Vogel takes the position that not every apparently convincing interpretation from the context should prevail over domestic law.[42] Only an interpretation based on relatively strong arguments should have predominance over recourse to domestic law. Klaus Vogel bases this position on the argument that Article 3 paragraph 2 of the OECD Model Tax Convention uses the phrase 'unless the context requires' and not 'unless the context yields no other, or absolutely no other, interpretation'.[43] In this author's opinion, this argument is not convincing.[44] It is not convincing to compare a phrase used by the OECD Model Tax Convention with another phrase which is not used by the OECD Model Tax Convention and to draw conclusions from existing differences. There is no indication why it should not be arguable that every convincing interpretation 'requires' its own relevance.[45] The wording leaves room for both alternative interpretations of the phrase 'unless the context otherwise requires'. Taking into account the above-mentioned object and purpose of the OECD Model Tax Convention, namely to avoid results which would make the tax treaty ineffective since

[40] M. Lang, 'Die Bedeutung des originär innerstaatlichen Rechts für die Auslegung von Doppelbesteuerungsabkommen (Art 3 Abs 2 OECD-MA)' in Burmester and Endres (eds), *Außensteuerrecht, Doppelbesteuerungsabkommen und EU-Recht im Spannungsverhältnis—FS Debatin* (1997) p. 283 (p. 287) (hereafter '*FS Debatin*').

[41] Bleckmann, *Grundprobleme,* p. 89; Debatin, (1995) *DB*, Beilage 23, p. 6; M. Lang, *Finanzierungen*, p. 25; Preuninger, *Rechtsprobleme des Funktionswandels deutscher Doppelbesteuerungsabkommen* (1980) p. 86.

[42] Vogel, *Double Taxation Conventions* (1997) Art 3 supra m.no. 71; Vogel and Prokisch, 'Die Auslegung von Doppelbesteuerungsabkommen—Generalbericht' (1993) *CDFI* LXXVIIIa, p. 55 (p. 81).

[43] Vogel, *Double Taxation Conventions* (1997) Art 3 supra m.no. 71; Vogel and Prokisch, (1993) *CDFI* LXXVIIIa, p. 81.

[44] M. Lang, in Gassner, M. Lang and Lechner (eds,) *Entwicklungen*, p. 35.

[45] Köck, '§ 1 des Entwurfs des DBA-Durchführungsgesetzes und die Auslegung von Doppelbesteuerungsabkommen' (1997) *SWI*, p. 382 (p. 387).

making reference to the domestic laws of the two Contracting States could lead to a different understanding of one and the same provision of a tax treaty in the two Contracting States, a solution which does not overemphasize the term 'requires' is convincing.[46] Historical arguments also suggest this solution. A provision comparable to Article 3 paragraph 2 of the OECD Model Tax Convention was first used in the tax treaty between the UK and the US, dating back to 1945.[47] Since then, such a provision can be found in almost all tax treaties. As Klaus Vogel and Rainer Prokisch hold, the reason for this success is not entirely clear.[48] Since this provision was inserted in the first OECD Model Tax Convention, dating back to 1963, without any reflection of its meaning, it cannot be assumed that this provision should deviate heavily from the otherwise applicable rules of interpretation of international treaties.[49] As the rules of interpretation of public international agreements require that such agreements be interpreted by paying attention to their context, meaning all historical, systematical and teleological aspects, the historical development is another argument for the interpretation which allows reference to domestic law only in situations where an interpretation deriving from the context cannot be established.[50]

Apparently, the system of the OECD Model Tax Convention does not support this approach. The phrase 'unless the context otherwise requires' is also used in Article 3 paragraph 1 of the OECD Model Tax Convention. The definitions contained in this provision may only be applied 'unless the context otherwise requires'. Treaty practice shows that, despite of this apparent restriction, the definitions contained in Article 3 paragraph 1 of the OECD Model Tax Convention are used. This could lead to the conclusion that the phrase 'unless the context otherwise requires' has almost no relevance at all. But this interpretation is not convincing. The wording of Article 3 paragraph 1 of the OECD Model Tax Convention can indicate an importance of the context of the treaty that even has predominance over definitions provided for in the treaty. Definitions should only be applicable if they are not in contradiction with an interpretation deriving from the context.[51]

Finally, it should not be ignored that the Commentary to the OECD Model Tax Convention contains a statement on Article 3 paragraph 2 of the OECD Model Tax Convention. This statement was inserted partly in 1992, and

---

[46] Gloria, *Das steuerliche Verständigungsverfahren und das Recht auf diplomatischen Schutz* (1988) p. 98; M. Lang, in Burmester and Endres (eds), *FS Debatin* (1997) p. 290; Schaumburg, *Internationales Steuerrecht* (1993) pp. 573 et seq.

[47] Avery Jones et al, (1984) *BTR*, p. 18.

[48] Vogel and Prokisch, (1993) *CDFI* LXXVIIIa, pp. 76 et seq.

[49] Vogel and Prokisch, (1993) *CDFI* LXXVIIIa, pp. 77.

[50] M. Lang, in Gassner, M. Lang and Lechner (eds), *Entwicklungen*, pp. 35 et seq.

[51] M. Lang, in Burmester and Endres (eds), *FS Debatin* (1997) pp. 289 et seq.

partly in 1995.[52] Therefore it can be of relevance for the interpretation of all tax treaties containing a provision comparable to Article 3 paragraph 2 of the OECD Model Tax Convention and negotiated and concluded after the revision of 1992 or 1995 of the Commentary. The statement reads as follows:[53]

'11.This paragraph provides a general rule of interpretation for terms used in the Convention but not defined therein. However, the question arises which legislation must be referred to in order to determine the meaning of terms not defined in the Convention, the choice being between the legislation in force when the Convention was signed or that in force when the Convention is being applied, i.e., when the tax is imposed. The Committee on Fiscal Affairs concluded that the latter interpretation should prevail, and in 1995 amended the Model to make this point explicitly.

12. However, paragraph 2 specifies that this applies only if the context does not require an alternative interpretation. The context is determined in particular by the intention of the Contracting States when signing the Convention as well as the meaning given to the term in question in the legislation of the other Contracting State (an implicit reference to the principle of reciprocity on which the Convention is based). The wording of the Article therefore allows the competent authorities some leeway.

13. Consequently, the wording of paragraph 2 provides a satisfactory balance between, on the one hand, the need to ensure the permanency of commitments entered into by States when signing a Convention (since a State should not be allowed to make a Convention partially inoperative by amending afterwards in its domestic law the scope of terms not defined in a Convention) and, on the other hand, the need to be able to apply the Convention in a convenient and practical way over time (the need to refer to outdated concepts should be avoided).

13.1. Paragraph 2 was amended in 1995 to conform its text more closely to the general and consistent understanding of Member States. For the purposes of paragraph 2, the meaning of any term not defined in the Convention may be ascertained by reference to the meaning it has for the purpose of any relevant provision of the domestic law of a Contracting State, whether or not a tax law. However, where a term is defined differently for the purposes of different laws of a Contracting State, the meaning given to that term for purposes of the laws imposing the taxes to which the Convention applies shall prevail over all others, including those given for the purposes of other tax laws. States that are

[52] M. Lang, in Burmester and Endres (eds), *FS Debatin* (1997) pp. 292 et seq.

[53] OECD, *MC Commentary*, Art 3 supra m.no. 11 et seq.

able to enter into mutual agreements (under the provisions of Article 25 and, in particular, Paragraph 3 thereof) that establish the meanings of terms not defined in the Convention should take those agreements into account in interpreting those terms'.

The above-mentioned statement focuses on the question if the reference to domestic law has to be understood as ambulatory or static, and this has been the subject of controversial discussion over a long period of time.[54] Therefore, other controversial issues are almost completely ignored. The drafters of the Commentary tried to clarify the meaning of the term 'context' but did not succeed. The remarks are misleading and not very helpful, as John F. Avery Jones has already pointed out.[55] The Commentary just mentions that the context 'is constituted in particular by the intention of the Contracting States when signing the Convention as well as the meaning given to the term in question in the legislation of the other Contracting State (an implicit reference to the principle of reciprocity on which the Convention is based)'. The Commentary emphasises two possible aspects which could be considered part of the context, but it does not give any reason why it selected those aspects. Therefore, the Commentary merely indicates that the term 'context' has a broad meaning.[56] This conclusion supports the findings as outlined above.

All the aforementioned arguments suggest that Article 3 paragraph 2 of the OECD Model Tax Convention merely emphasises that the OECD Model Tax Convention has primarily to be interpreted from its context. Where this approach does not lead to a result recourse may be made to the domestic law of the Contracting State applying the treaty. Since the term 'context' includes all available historical, systematical and teleological aspects, it will almost

---

54 Avery Jones et al, (1984) *BTR*, p. 14 et seq. and p. 90 et seq.; Ault, in Alpert and van Raad (eds), *Essays* (1993) pp. 67 et seq,; Gröhs and Herbst, (1986) *ZfV*, p. 25 footnote 84; K. van Raad, '1992 Additions to Articles 3 (2) (Interpretation) and 24 (Non-Discrimination) of the 1992 OECD Model and Commentary' (1992) *Intertax*, p. 671 (pp. 672 et seq.); Koja, 'Zur Frage der verfassungsrechtlichen Zulässigkeit statischer und dynamischer Verweisungen' (1979) *ÖJZ*, p. 29 (pp. 29 et seq.); M. Lang, 'Verfassungsrechtliche Bedenken gegen die Verweisungsnormen in Doppelbesteuerungsabkommen' (1989) *ÖStZ*, p. 11 (pp. 11 et seq.); M. Lang, 'Die Interpretation des Doppelbesteuerungsabkommens zwischen Deutschland und Österreich' (1992) *RIW*, p. 573 (pp. 574 et seq.); Sinclair et al, 'Interpretation of Tax Treaties' (1986) *BIFD*, p. 75 (pp. 75 et seq.); Vogel, *Double Taxation Conventions* (1997) Introduction supra m.no. 124 b et seq.; Widmann, 'Zurechnungsänderungen und Umqualifikationen durch das nationale Recht in ihrem Verhältnis zum DBA-Recht' in Vogel (ed.), *Grundfragen des internationalen Steuerrechts*, p. 235 (p. 251).

55 Avery Jones, (1993) *ET*, pp. 253 et seq.

56 M. Lang, in Gassner, M. Lang and Lechner (eds), *Entwicklungen*, pp. 34 et seq.; Vogel, *Double Taxation Conventions* (1997) Art 3 supra m.no. 72; Vogel and Prokisch, (1993) *CDFI* LXXVIIIa, p. 82.

always be possible to establish an interpretation which is guided by the context. Recourse to domestic law is rarely necessary.

Obviously this result does not lead to the conclusion that domestic law is completely irrelevant. The OECD Model Tax Convention and many bilateral tax treaties contain a lot of explicit or implicit references to domestic law.[57] In these situations, recourse to domestic law is not made because the context does not 'otherwise require': it is the context that requires the relevance of domestic law. As domestic tax law allocates all taxable income to a 'taxpayer', however defined, this taxpayer has to be entitled to the treaty benefits.[58] Otherwise, the tax treaties would not fulfil their function. The same is true for the taxable income as such.[59] Tax treaties force the Contracting States to reduce their tax base under certain conditions. Therefore, tax treaties have to make reference to those provisions of domestic law which define the tax base. Whenever the OECD Model Tax Convention or a bilateral tax treaty uses the term 'income' or 'profits', it refers to domestic tax law provisions. There are also other cases of reference to domestic law, especially in tax treaties deviating from the OECD Model Tax Convention. In some tax treaties, for example, definitions used in the domestic law of one of the Contracting States are used deliberately.[60] In these cases, tax treaty negotiators often want to make very clear that a certain tax treaty provision should have the same meaning as the model provision under domestic law. All these situations have in common the principle that domestic law is relevant for treaty interpretation, not because 'the context' does not 'otherwise require', but because the context indeed requires.

In the light of these findings, there is no real need to resolve conflicts of qualification by assuming that the State of residence is bound by the qualification of the State of source. The OECD Report develops a scheme to resolve conflicts which are created by its own assumptions. If the Committee paid more attention to the 'context' of a certain tax treaty when interpreting its provisions, conflicts of qualification could be avoided from the beginning. It is disappointing that the Committee does not focus on the examination how to avoid conflicts of qualification, but accepts premises which provoke conflicts of qualification that the Committee attempts to later resolve through questionable means, as will be discussed later.

---

57 E.g., Art 6 para 2 and Art 10 para 3 of the OECD Model Tax Convention.

58 Stoll, *Steuerschuldverhältnis*, pp. 162 et seq.

59 Debatin, (1995) *DB*, Beilage 23, p. 4; M. Lang, *Finanzierungen*, pp. 73 et seq.; M. Lang, *Doppelbesteuerungsabkommen*, p. 102.

60 Debatin, (1995) *DB*, Beilage 23, p. 5; M. Lang, *Finanzierungen*, p. 32; M. Lang, (1999) *SWI*, p. 68.

3. The Avoidance of Double Taxation and Double Non-Taxation as Object and Purpose of the OECD Model Tax Convention

One other premise the Committee takes is that the object and purpose of the OECD Model Tax Convention is to avoid double taxation. The OECD Report contains a few statements which indicate that this is the underlying premise. In paragraph 53, for example, the Committee explicitly states that it 'views the outcome in the above examples as resulting from an application of the Convention: to eliminate double taxation ...'.

The Report also explicitly mentions that non-taxation has to be avoided. Some statements contained in the Report indicate that solutions leading to non-taxation are in contradiction to the aims and the purposes of the OECD Model Tax Convention.[61] Paragraph 52 states, for example, that part of the 'basic purposes of the Convention' is 'to prevent double non-taxation'.

It is clear however that the avoidance of double taxation is not in contradiction with the OECD Model Tax Convention. But that does not necessarily mean that a specific interpretation of a provision of the OECD Model Tax Convention is only in accordance with the treaty if double taxation can be avoided. It has to be borne in mind that tax treaties do not attempt to avoid double taxation in general, but only within their scope. This means that cases of double taxation not covered by the scope of the treaty have to be accepted. Cases of so-called 'economic double taxation', for example, are not solved by the tax treaty. The only restriction is based on Article 9 OECD Model Tax Convention, which provides that only profits resulting out of conditions made or imposed between associated enterprises may be adjusted on an arm's length basis. This means that the OECD Model Tax Convention does not prevent the contracting partners from allocating the income to different taxpayers in other situations not covered by Article 9 OECD Model Tax Convention. Therefore, it is not convincing to argue that every tax treaty provision must be interpreted in a way that double taxation is avoided. This assumption is only true in situations covered by the tax treaty. Therefore, the avoidance of double taxation may only be the result of the interpretation of a certain tax treaty provision and must not operate as the underlying premise in every situation.

On the other hand, the avoidance of non-taxation is not part of the object and purpose of the OECD Model Tax Convention either. It is true that tax treaties are not primarily concluded to create situations of non-taxation. However, it is clear that the application of a tax treaty provision can very easily lead to the result of double non-taxation. If one Contracting State is prevented from exercising its taxing rights according to the treaty, and the other Contracting

[61] OECD, supra note 1, paras 44, 52, 109.

State does not impose taxes because of domestic restrictions or because of a lack of domestic provisions, it is completely clear and unquestioned that double non-taxation is the result of the application of the tax treaty. This has to be accepted, unless according to a specific 'subject-to-tax-clause' the exemption in one Contracting State depends on the fact that the other Contracting State exercises its taxing rights.[62] As the OECD Model Tax Convention does not contain such a 'subject-to-tax-clause', one cannot argue against a certain interpretation of a treaty provision that the object and purpose of the treaty make it necessary to avoid double non-taxation situations.

62 OECD, *MC Commentary*, Art 1 supra m.no. 17.

III. The Entitlement of Partnerships to Treaty Benefits

1. Partnerships as Persons who are Residents of one Contracting State

The OECD Report contains a chapter which specifically deals with the question concerning as to when a partnership is entitled to the benefits of a tax Convention. The introduction to this chapter reads as follows:

27. Where income is derived from a particular State, the determination of the tax consequences in that State will first require the application of the domestic tax laws of that State. It is the provisions of these laws that will determine who may be subjected to tax on that income in that State. The provisions of tax Conventions, however, may then intervene to restrict or eliminate the taxing rights originating from domestic law where a person, usually but not necessarily the taxpayer identified under domestic law, is eligible for the benefits of the tax Convention in relation to that income.

This introduction can be supported to a certain extent. It is reasonable to suggest that whoever applies a tax treaty should start by applying domestic law.[63] Whoever follows this suggestion can be certain that he avoids a common mistake in practice, namely concluding that only because a tax treaty grants the taxing right in a certain situation to a Contracting State, this taxing right is exercised by this State in any case.[64] Such a conclusion would not be correct, because it certainly depends on the domestic law whether taxing rights provided for by a tax treaty are exercised. Starting with domestic law one can avoid this incorrect conclusion. However, this does not necessarily mean that it would be incorrect to commence one's analysis by looking at the tax treaty first.[65] Keeping in mind that tax treaties must not create a tax liability, nothing prevents one looking at the tax treaty first. On the other hand, it is also clear that tax treaties contain some provisions which

---

[63] M. Lang, *Einführung in das Recht der Doppelbesteuerungsabkommen* (1997) supra m.no. 142 et seq. (hereafter 'Einführung'); Loukota, 'Vermeidung von Irrwegen bei der DBA-Auslegung' (1998) *SWI*, p. 559 (p. 561).

[64] M. Lang, 'Die Einwirkung der Doppelbesteuerungsabkommen auf das innerstaatliche Recht' (1988) *FJ*, 72 (75); M. Lang, *Einführung* (1997) supra m.no. 40 et seq.

[65] Debatin, (1995) *DB*, Beilage 23, p. 2; Debatin, 'Replik zu K. Vogel' (1986) *DB*, p. 510 (pp. 512 et seq.); M. Lang, (1988) *FJ*, p. 72; M. Lang, 'Irrwege der DBA Auslegung am Beispiel der Besteuerung von Lehrbeauftragten' (1998) *SWI*, p. 508 (p. 513); M. Lang, (1999) *SWI*, pp. 62 et seq.; Vogel, 'Doppelbesteuerungsabkommen und ihre Auslegung' (1982) *StuW*, p. 111 (pp. 118 et seq.); Vogel, 'Zu einigen Fragen des internationalen Steuerrechts' (1986) *DB*, p. 507 (pp. 508 et seq.); whereas Loukota, (1998) *SWI*, p. 561 adopts a different opinion.

refer to domestic law, as shown above. In interpreting such a tax treaty provision, one has to make recourse to domestic law as far as this reference applies. Therefore, the interpretation of those tax treaty provisions determining the person who is entitled to the tax treaty benefits, requires a consideration of the domestic law provisions which constitute the person who is the taxpayer. As shown above, this is one of the cases where tax treaty provisions refer to domestic law. In general the OECD Reports shares this opinion, as it mentions that 'usually ... the taxpayer identified under domestic law is eligible for the benefits of the tax Convention in relation to that income'.[66] At the same time, the OECD Report makes the exception that is 'not necessarily' the case[67], failing to identify the conditions under which such an exception may be applicable. No reasoning is given for the opinion that there might be exceptions to the general rule. The lack of reasoning in this paragraph is deplorable, since many conclusions drawn in further paragraphs of this Report are based on the opinion that treaty benefits need not necessarily be granted to persons who are residents of one of the Contracting States.

However, the statements contained in the following paragraph can be entirely supported:

28. The clear rule of Article 1 of the Model Tax Convention is that only persons who are residents of the Contracting States are entitled to the benefits of the tax Convention entered into by these States. Where income is earned by a partnership, the issue of whether the partnership itself is entitled to the benefits of the Convention will depend on whether the partnership qualifies as person who is a resident of a Contracting State under the definitions of Article 3 and of paragraph 1 of Article 4.

In a convincing way the OECD Report—examining the current version of the Commentary—concludes that the term 'person' may also cover partnerships:

29. For a partnership, entitlement to treaty benefits will therefore first depend on whether it qualifies as a 'person'. Subparagraph 1 (a) of Article 3 of the Model defines a 'person' for purposes of the Convention as 'an individual, a company and any other body of persons'. Paragraph 2 of the Commentary on Article 3 provides:

> 'The definition of the term 'person' given in subparagraph (a) is not exhaustive and should be read as indicating that the term 'person' is used in a very wide sense (compare especially Articles 1 and 4). The definition explicitly mentions individuals, companies and other bodies of persons. From the meaning assigned to the term 'company'

66 OECD, supra note 1, para 27.
67 OECD, supra note 1, para 27.

by the definition contained in subparagraph (b) it follows that, in addition, the term 'person' includes any entity which, although itself not a body of persons, is treated as a body corporate for tax purposes. Thus, e.g., a foundation (*foundation, Stiftung*) may fall within the meaning of the term 'person'. Special considerations for the application of the Convention to partnerships are found in paragraphs 2 to 6 of the Commentary on Article 1'.

30. The Commentary on Article 1, however, does not discuss the issue of whether a partnership is a 'person' within the meaning of Article 3. While the practices of Member countries are not entirely uniform in this respect, the Committee has determined that partnerships should be considered to be 'persons' within the meaning of the definition found in Article 3. In most countries, partnerships (as well as the individual partners) will be considered to be 'persons' within the meaning of Article 3 either because the partnerships fall within the definition of company or because they are bodies of persons. The Committee has therefore decided to delete the last sentence of paragraph 2 of the Commentary on Article 3 and to replace it with the following sentence:

    'Partnerships will also be considered to be 'persons' either because they fall within the definition of 'company' or, where this is not the case, because they constitute other bodies of persons'.

31. The Committee has noted, however, that the definition of the term 'national' in subdivision 1 (f)(ii) of Article 3 may give rise to an implication that partnerships are not 'persons' for purposes of the Convention. That definition provides that the term 'national' includes 'any legal person, partnership or association deriving its status as such from the laws in force in a Contracting State'. As a matter of grammar and logic, a specific term that is included within a broader general term is not ordinarily given separate mention in a list that contains the general term.

32. In order to avoid any confusion that may result from that definition, the Committee has agreed to add the following paragraph to the Commentary on Article 3:

    'The separate mention of partnerships in subparagraph 1 (f) is not inconsistent with the status of a partnership as a person under subparagraph 1 (a). Under the domestic laws of some countries, it is possible for an entity to be a 'person' but not a 'legal person' for tax purposes. The explicit statement is necessary to avoid confusion'.

As far as the qualification of a partnership as a 'person' is concerned, the OECD Report's conclusion is convincing. It seems obvious that a 'person' defined in Article 3 paragraph 1 subparagraph (a) of the OECD Model Tax Convention is something different than a 'legal person' mentioned in Article

3 paragraph 1 subparagraph (f) of the OECD Model Tax Convention.[68] There was not even a need for clarification. However, the amendment to the Commentary does not create a new meaning of the term 'person', compared to the previous version of the Commentary. Therefore tax treaties having the same wording as the OECD Model Tax Convention and concluded before the suggested amendment to the Commentary was made, may be interpreted in the same way. Nevertheless, this example shows that mere clarifications of the Commentary can easily be misleading because, it is always uncertain whether such a mere clarification is really no more than a mere clarification. Therefore, so-called clarifications should be avoided as they usually raise more questions than they answer.[69]

Subsequently, the OECD Report deals with the question whether a partnership can be considered a 'resident of a Contracting State'. In doing so, the OECD Report reads as follows:

33. Paragraph 3 of the Commentary on Article 1 deals specifically with the problem of whether a partnership qualifies as a 'resident' for treaty purposes. The Commentary states:

    'First, the question arises whether a partnership as such may invoke the provisions of the Convention. Where a partnership is treated as a company or taxed in the same way, it may reasonably be argued that the partnership is a resident of the Contracting State taxing the partnership on the grounds mentioned in paragraph 1 of Article 4 and therefore, falling under the scope of the Convention, is entitled to the benefits of the Convention. In the other instances mentioned in paragraph 2 above, the application of the Convention to the partnership as such might be refused, at least if no special rule is provided for in the Convention covering partnerships'.

34. The Committee discussed this paragraph and concluded that its analysis is correct. If the State in which a partnership has been organised treats that partnership as fiscally transparent, then the partnership is not 'liable to tax' in the State within the meaning of Article 4, and so cannot be a resident for purposes of the Convention. Although inconvenient at times (e.g., paragraph 89 below), there appears to be little scope for a contrary argument under the current wording of Article 4.

35. To clarify this point, the Committee has agreed to delete the last sentence of paragraph 3 of the Commentary on Article 1 and to replace it with the following sentences:

---

68 OECD, supra note 1, para 32.

69 M. Lang, 'Die Bedeutung der 1995 erfolgten Änderungen des OECD-Musterabkommens und des OECD-Steuerausschusses für die Doppelbesteuerungsabkommen' in Lang, Loukota and Lüthi (eds), *Die Weiterwicklung des OECD-Musterabkommens* (1996) p. 25 (pp. 51 et seq.).

> 'Where, however, a partnership is treated as fiscally transparent in a State, the partnership is not "liable to tax" in that State within the meaning of paragraph 1 of Article 4, and so cannot be a resident thereof for purposes of the Convention. In such a case, the application of the Convention to the partnership as such would be refused, unless a special rule covering partnerships were provided for in the Convention. Where the application of the Convention is so refused, the partners are entitled, with respect to their share of the income of the partnership, to the benefits provided by the Conventions entered into by the countries of which they are residents to the extent that they are liable to tax therein on that share of the partnership's income (compare paragraphs 8.2 and 8.3 of the Commentary on Article 4)'.

Again, it is doubtful whether there was really a need to change and amend the Commentary. Although the previous version of the Commentary did not explicitly mention that partners are entitled to their share of income of the partnership provided by the tax treaty, this result was fully accepted. However, the reason why the OECD Report suggests an amendment of the Commentary seems to be related to the reference to other paragraphs of the Commentary contained in the above-mentioned paragraph. Obviously, it should be made clear that the relevant statements are contained in other paragraphs, which will be dealt with separately.

Subsequently, the OECD Report recognizes that the really relevant question deciding the tax treaty treatment of partnerships is how to understand the phrase 'liable to tax' contained in Article 4 paragraph 1 of the OECD Model Tax Convention.

37. The Committee discussed in detail how the concept of 'liable to tax' should be understood in the context of different systems for taxing partnerships' income. The Committee first discussed cases where domestic tax laws create intermediary situations where a partnership is partly treated as a taxable unit and partly disregarded for tax purposes. While this may create practical difficulties with respect to a very limited number of partnerships, it is a more important problem in the case of other entities such as trusts. For this reason, the Committee decided to deal with this issue in the context of follow-up work to this Report.

38. The Committee then examined two common approaches to taxation of partnerships. In many countries, the tax laws provide that income derived by a partnership from a particular source must be computed at the partnership level as if the partnership were a distinct taxpayer. Each partner is then allocated his share of that income which retains its character and is added to his income for purposes of determining his taxable income. His taxable income, including his share of the partner-

ship's income is then reduced by the personal allowances and deductions to which he is entitled and tax is then determined, assessed and paid at a partner's level. In such cases, it is clear that the partnership is not itself liable to tax.

39. In other countries, the income and the tax payable is computed in a similar way, but the tax payable by the partners is then aggregated at the level of the partnership which is then assessed for the total amount of the tax. In these cases, the assessment of the tax in the hands of the partnership is a collection technique that does not change the fact that the tax payable on the income of the partnership is determined at each partner's level taking into account the other income of that partner, the personal allowances to which he is entitled and the tax rate applicable to him (which may vary depending on his total income or his nature). In such cases, the partnership is also not liable to tax.

40. The Committee agreed that for purposes of determining whether a partnership is liable to tax, the real question is whether the amount of tax payable on the partnership income is determined in relation to the personal characteristics of the partners (whether the partners are taxable or not, what other income do they have, what are the personal allowances to which they are entitled, what is the tax rate applicable to them). If the answer to that question is yes, then the partnership should not itself be considered to be liable to tax. The fact that the income is computed at the level of the partnership before being allocated to the partners, that the tax is technically paid by the partnership or that it is assessed on the partnership as described in the preceding paragraph will not change that result.

41. The fact that a partnership may be said to be liable to tax in a State will not, however, be sufficient for it to be considered a resident of that State for purposes of tax Conventions. Paragraph 1 of Article 4 also required that the liability to tax in that State be caused by one of the criteria listed therein (e.g., residence, domicile etc.). Thus, for a partnership to be a resident of a Contracting State, it has to be liable to tax in that State by reason of one of these criteria.

42. The provisions of tax Conventions will apply differently depending on whether or not a partnership qualifies as a resident. Where a partnership does not so qualify because it is the partners who are liable to tax on the partnership's income, the income derived by the partnership should be considered to keep the nature and source that it had in the hands of the partnership for purposes of the provisions of a tax Convention. This corresponds to the situation that is generally provided for under the domestic laws of the countries that do not treat partnerships as taxable entities. Thus, where a partnership is treated as transparent for purposes of tax Conventions because it is the partners rather than the partnership

who are liable to tax on the partnership's income, that income will, when applying the relevant Convention, keep the nature and source that it had in the hands of the partnership for purposes of taxation in the hands of the partners.

The deliberations of the OECD Report in that respect are very important. The OECD Report implicitly admits that it is not that simple to qualify a partnership as transparent or non-transparent. A few years ago, Le Gall has shown in his General Report for the International Fiscal Association (IFA), that partnerships can be treated in various ways.[70] There is a range of different tax treatments applicable to partnerships. According to many jurisdictions, partnerships are not treated in the same way as taxable entities, but on the other hand are not completely treated as transparent. It is therefore very difficult to draw the borderline. The OECD Report tries to solve this problem by explicitly mentioning some situations in which a partnership qualifies as a resident person and in which it does not. However, the OECD Report refrains from giving reasons for the position it takes. Therefore the statements contained in the OECD Report are not as helpful as they could have been. Furthermore, the OECD Report fails to deal with a range of situations. Nevertheless, one has to admit that these questions are very difficult; it is a progressive approach for the OECD Report not to ignore this issue completely.

2. The Relevance of the Tax Treatment in the State of Residence

The main part of the OECD Report focuses on cross-border situations where in at least one Contracting State a partnership does not qualify as a resident. The OECD Report summarizes its position by stating 'that the partners should be entitled to the benefits provided by the Conventions entered into by the countries of which they are residents to the extent that they are liable to tax on their share of the partnership income in those countries'.[71]

It has to be noted that the Committee is of the opinion that the tax treatment in the other Contracting State is relevant for the entitlement to treaty benefits. Only persons who are residents of the other Contracting State may claim treaty benefits in the source State. To qualify as a resident, it is necessary to be 'liable to tax' in this Contracting State. Furthermore, it is not enough to be 'liable to tax' as such, the residents also have to be 'liable to tax on their share of the partnership income'. This approach comes close to a 'subject-to-tax-clause' and can be challenged in several ways. These are as follows.

First, there is no reason why the term 'liable to tax' contained in Article 4 paragraph 1 of the OECD Model Tax Convention should be interpreted as

70 Le Gall, (1995) *CDFI* LXXXa, p. 657 (pp. 665 et seq.).

71 OECD, supra note 1, para 47.

suggested by the Committee. Since the OECD Model Tax Convention does not contain a general 'subject-to-tax-clause', the imposition of taxes is not a requirement for the application of a tax treaty. Tax treaties are even applicable if one Contracting State does not exercise the taxing rights provided for in the tax treaty. The tax exemption of income in one State does not prevent the taxpayer from claiming tax treaty benefits in the other Contracting State. The effects of a tax exemption are the same as not imposing taxes from the start or not allocating the income to the person. Therefore, it is not convincing to assume that tax treaty benefits may only be granted if the taxpayers 'are liable to tax on their share of the partnership income'.

Furthermore, there is no reason why the tax treatment in the *other* Contracting State should be relevant at all for the entitlement to treaty benefits in the source State in a situation where a partnership is treated differently in both States. According to a well-accepted principle of treaty application, tax treaties restrict the imposition of taxes provided for by domestic tax law. Therefore, it is the domestic taxpayer who is entitled to the treaty benefits. If the taxes are imposed on the taxpayer, the tax treaty can only properly function if the same taxpayer is entitled to the treaty benefits. Therefore, it makes sense to assume that it is not up to the residence State to decide who shall be entitled to the treaty benefits in the source State. It is the source State that decides on the taxpayer's status. Therefore, this decision should be considered relevant for treaty application purposes.

If the other Contracting State does not treat the partnership as a taxable entity, it seems that the partnership cannot be considered a resident of this other Contracting State. However, as Klaus Vogel has pointed out, to qualify as a resident it is not necessary to be actually taxed in that State.[72] It is therefore sufficient if the partnership has a certain link to the State of residence which would lead to unlimited taxation there if the partnership were a taxable entity.[73] If this partnership is established under the law of that other Contracting State, and has its seat and place of management there, it will more than likely fulfil the criteria necessary to qualify for being treated as a resident, even if it is not treated as a taxable entity by the State of residence.

However, that does not mean that the actual tax treatment in the State of residence is completely irrelevant. On the contrary, claiming treaty benefits in the State of residence requires being treated as a taxable entity there. Therefore, one has to distinguish between the tax treaty treatment in the State of residence and in the State of source. Claiming treaty benefits in the State

---

[72] Vogel, *Double Taxation Conventions* (1997) Art 4 supra m.no. 25.

[73] M. Lang, 'Die abkommensrechtliche Behandlung von ausländischen Personengesellschaften mit Steuersubjektivität im Ausland' in Kleineidam (ed.), *Unternehmenspolitik und internationale Besteuerung: Festschrift für Lutz Fischer zum 60. Geburtstag* (1999) p. 713 (pp. 716 et seq.) (hereafter '*FS Lutz Fischer*'); Vogel, *Double Taxation Conventions* (1997) Art 4 supra m.no. 25.

of source, such as applying a withholding tax reduction there, requires treatment as a taxable entity there. Claiming treaty benefits in the State of residence, such as exempting foreign income or crediting foreign taxes, however, requires treatment as a taxable entity in that State.

The Committee obviously assumes that being a resident in at least one of the Contracting States is still a requirement for the treaty application. However, it is not at all clear if this is still true. The OECD Model Tax Convention contains a non-discrimination clause for permanent establishments. Therefore, under certain conditions the taxation of permanent establishments which an enterprise of a Contracting State has in the other Contracting State must not be levied less favourably in that other State than the taxation levied on enterprises of the other State carrying on the same activities.[74] Although it is not completely clear from the Commentary, this could lead to the result that a permanent establishment may claim the same treaty benefits as a resident in that State.[75] Of course, no treaty benefits have to be granted by third countries, since a bilateral treaty cannot create obligations for a third party. However, these permanent establishments might apply the exemption, or the credit method, as if they were residents of that State. In respect to partnerships, one has to keep in mind that partnerships might constitute permanent establishments for the partners.[76] Therefore, partnerships might also claim treaty benefits, by virtue of the non-discrimination clause for permanent establishments. It is true that according to the Commentary, this position does not derive directly from the wording of the OECD Model Tax Convention.[77] However, since these questions are heavily discussed among scholars and practioners in many countries, it is deplorable that the Committee has completely ignored these issues. It would not be at all surprising if courts took the position that partnerships could claim treaty benefits. Under this assumption, most of the statements contained in the Report seem to be outdated. The same is true for partnerships established in EU Member States, having partners who are residents of other EU Member States. As long as the partnership constitutes a permanent establishment for the partners, it is entitled to the treaty benefits of the treaties concluded by the State where the partnership is located, as far as the State where the partnership is located is concerned. The freedoms enshrined in the EC Treaty do not leave room for another solution, which should be clear after the *Saint Gobain* decision of the European Court of Justice.[78]

---

[74] Art 24 para 3 OECD MC.

[75] OECD, *MC Commentary*, Art 24 supra m.no. 21.

[76] Tumpel, 'Die Beteiligung an einer Personengesellschaft als Bertriebstätte des Gesellschafters' in Gassner, M. Lang and Lechner (eds), *Die Betriebstätte im Recht der Doppelbesteuerungsabkommen* (1998) p. 145 (pp. 150 et seq.).

[77] OECD, *MC Commentary*, Art 24 supra m.no. 19 et seq.

[78] See ECJ Case, *Saint Gobain*, No. C-307/97 [1999].

3. The Relevance of the Tax Treatment in the State of Source

As indicated before, the Committee takes the position that the tax treatment in the State of residence is relevant for the entitlement to the treaty benefits in the State of source. Surprisingly, as far as qualification conflicts are concerned, the Committee takes the opposite position. In this respect the OECD Report reads as follows:

102. The Committee agreed that, in addressing conflicts of qualification problems faced by the State of residence, a useful starting point is the recognition of the principle that the domestic law of the State applying its tax governs all matters regarding how and in the hands of whom an item of income is taxed. The effect of tax Conventions can only be to limit or eliminate the taxing rights of the Contracting States. In the case of the source State, the right to tax items of income is limited by provisions based on Article 6 through to 21 of the Model Tax Convention. In the case of the residence State, while provisions based on Articles such as 8 and 19 might be relevant, the primary restriction would arise from the provisions of the Article on Elimination of Double Taxation (Article 23 in the Model Tax Convention), by which the residence State agrees to either exempt income that the source State may tax under the Convention or to give a credit for the tax levied by the source State on that item of income.

103. When taxing an item of income, the source State therefore applies its domestic law, subject to the restrictions and limitations imposed on it by the provision of its tax Conventions. The way that the State of residence qualifies an item of income for treaty purposes has no relevance on how and in the hands of whom the State of source taxes that item of income. The reverse, however, is not true. The way the State of residence eliminates double taxation will depend, to some extent, on how the Convention has been applied by the State of source.

104. The wording of Article 23 of the OECD Model Tax Convention is crucial in that respect. That article requires that relief be granted, either through the exemption or credit system, where an item of income may be taxed 'in accordance with the provisions of the Convention'. Thus, the State of residence has a treaty obligation to apply the exemption or credit method vis-à-vis any item of income where the tax Convention authorizes taxation of that item of income by the State of source.

105. The meaning of the phrase 'in accordance with the provision of this Convention, may be taxed' needs to be clarified in that respect. Where, due to differences in the domestic law between the State of source and the State of residence, the former applies, with respect to a particular item of income, provisions of the Convention that are different from those that the State of residence would have applied to the same item

> of income, the income is still being taxed in accordance with the provisions of the Convention, in this case as interpreted by the State of source. In such a case, therefore, Article 23 requires that relief from double taxation be granted by the State of residence notwithstanding the conflict of qualification resulting from these differences in domestic law.

Such an interpretation of the OECD Model Tax Convention assumes that the relevant treaty provision cannot be interpreted from its context. According to the Report, the residence State shall only be bound by the treatment in the source State if the source State has to apply its domestic law because, according to Article 3 paragraph 2 of the OECD Model Tax Convention, the context does not otherwise require. However, if an interpretation from the context is at stake, the position taken in the State of source is not binding for the State of residence. The State of residence is not obliged to follow a different—in her point of view, wrong—interpretation applied by the State of source. Therefore, the question will very often arise if recourse to the domestic law of the State of source has to be made, because the context does not otherwise require or if one can arrive at an interpretation derived from the context. Only in the first case has the State of residence to follow the State of source's treatment. Therefore, it is in the interest of the State of source to apply his domestic law to enlarge his tax base. At the same time, it is in the interest of the State of residence to arrive at an interpretation derived from the context, so that the State of residence is not obliged to follow the State of source's qualification and keep his own taxing rights. As will be shown later, even the examples chosen by the Committee do not necessarily require to refer to domestic law, but can be solved from the context of the treaty. Therefore, the approach suggested by the Committee will not solve existing qualification conflicts but will provoke further qualification conflicts.

However, there is no reason to follow the approach suggested by the Committee. First, qualification conflicts do not arise if both countries stick to a context-interpretation. Secondly, the qualification conflict will not be solved, unless *both States* agree that a certain interpretation cannot be derived from the context. As far as the State of residence has in mind concerning the maintenance of its taxing rights, this is very unlikely.[79]

There is even less reason to insert a provision in the OECD Model Tax Convention, as a consequence of which the State of residence is even bound to the qualification of the State of source if double non-taxation results from

[79] See also Opinion of the Joint Tax Commitee of the Federal Chamber of Tax Consultants (Germany), the Austrian Chamber of Chartered Accountants and Tax Advisers and the Swiss Institute of Certified Accountants and Tax Consultants (D-A-CH Tax Committee) on the Subject of Qualification Disputes (1999) *Intertax*, p. 172.

different interpretations of the Convention or of the facts. If the Contracting States were forced to arrive at a common interpretation of the Convention and the facts instead, the object and the purpose would be better served. Nevertheless, the OECD CFA decided to insert a new provision in the OECD Model Tax Convention:

113. The Committee decided that the best way of addressing such cases of double non-taxation would be through a provision, to be added to Article 23A, that would provide that the residence State does not have to grant exemption in these cases. Such a provision would deal with cases of double non-taxation resulting from different interpretations of the provisions of the Convention or of the facts. The Committee therefore decided that the following paragraph 4 be added to Article 23A of the Model Tax Convention:

> '4. The provisions of paragraph 1 shall not apply to income derived or owned by a resident of a Contracting State where the other Contracting State applies the provisions of this Convention to exempt such income or capital from tax or applies the provisions of paragraph 2 of Article 10 or 11 to such income'.

IV. The Examples Explaining OECD's Conception on the Entitlement of Partnerships to Treaty Benefits

1. Example 1

P is a partnership established in State P. A and B are P's partners who reside in State P. Both States P and S treat P as a transparent entity, P derives interest income from State S that is not attributable to a permanent establishment in State S.

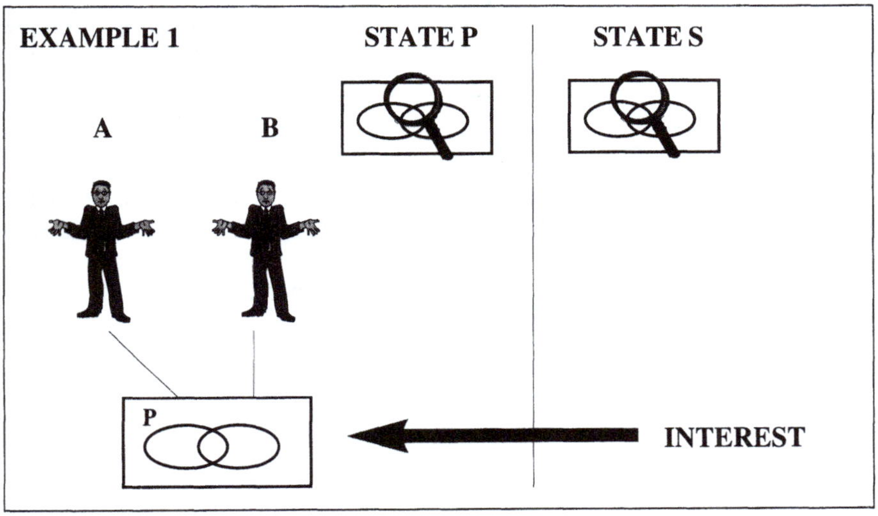

48. In this example, State S would be likely to determine that, under its domestic law, the relevant taxpayers are A and B. After applying its domestic law, it would then consider the application of the S-P tax Convention and, in particular, Article 11. Under paragraph 1 of Article 11, the Article applies to interest that is 'paid to a resident of another State'. In these circumstances, the income is appropriately viewed as 'paid' to A and B since it is to them and not to the partnership that the income is allocated for the purposes of determining their tax liability in State P. They thus have derived the income in the sense which is relevant for the application of the treaty. In effect, the source State would view the income as having 'flowed through' the transparent partnership of the partners who are liable to tax on that income in the State of their residence.

Example 1 serves as an introductory example. It describes a situation where both countries, the State of residence and the State of source, apply a look-through approach. The solution suggested by the authors of the OECD Report can be supported. Nevertheless, attention should be paid to the arguments leading to that conclusion. According to the OECD Report, the partners are entitled to the treaty benefits because the income of the partnership is allocated to the partners in their State of residence. It is not the tax treatment in the State of source which is relevant according to the OECD Report. This means that irrespective of the tax treatment in the State of residence the partners should be entitled to the treaty benefits as long as the income of the partnership is allocated to them according to the domestic law of the State of residence. Even if the partnership would be considered a taxable entity according to the domestic law of the State of source, the partners would be entitled to the treaty benefits. The underlying assumption is obviously that a resident of the State of residence may be entitled to the treaty benefits in the State of source even, if according to the domestic law of the State of source, this resident is not liable to tax. This premise cannot be shared, as argued above.

The OECD Report focuses on the tax treaty treatment in the State of source in this example and ignores the question if double taxation can be avoided in the State of residence. The answer would be in the affirmative, in this author's view, that State P taxes the partners and therefore will credit the tax levied in State S, if there is any.

2. Example 2

P is an entity established in State P. A and B are P's partners who reside in State R. States R, P and S all treat P as a transparent entity. P derives interest income from State S that is not attributable to a permanent establishment in State S.

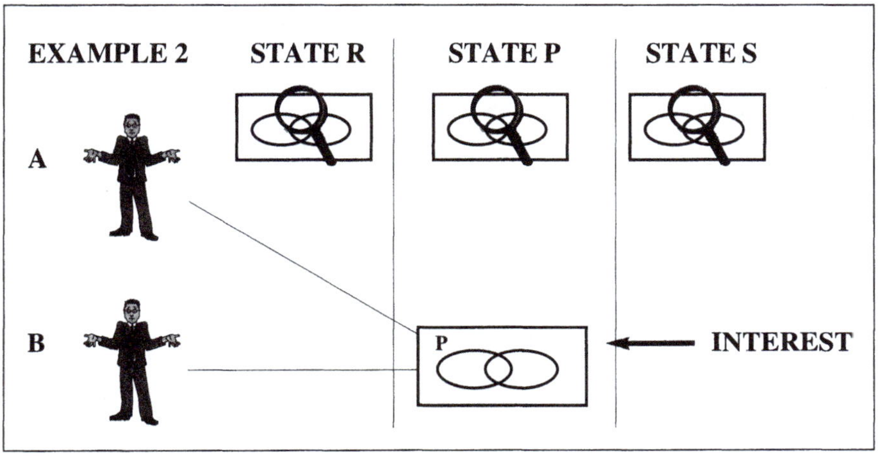

49. This example extends the basic principle illustrated in Example 1 above to a more complex situation involving three countries and two Conventions. As regards State S, again it will begin the analysis by determining that under its domestic law, the relevant taxpayers are A and B. In applying the S-R treaty, it would likewise determine that A and B have been allocated the income by State R and thus are liable to tax on that income for the purposes of determining that A and B have been allocated the income by State R and thus are liable to tax on that income for the purposes of determining their entitlement to benefits under the Convention. By contrast, P may not claim benefits under the S-P Convention since it is not a resident of State P (it is not liable to tax in that State).

50. Such cases, in which the partners are not residents in the State where the partnership has been organized, raise additional difficulties for tax authorities wishing to verify a taxpayer's entitlement to treaty benefits. Clearly, States should not be expected to grant the benefits of tax Conventions in cases where they cannot verify whether a person is truly entitled to these benefits. Thus, the application of the provisions of the S-R Convention will be conditional on State S being able to obtain all the necessary information.

Again, the OECD Report emphasises that the income of the partnership is allocated to the partners A and B by the domestic law of State R. According to the OECD Report, it is not the allocation by State S of the income to the partners A and B which is decisive. As advocated above, it is not convincing to assume that the entitlement of the partners A and B to tax treaty benefits should depend on the tax treatment in State R.

Furthermore, this approach applied by the OECD Report causes other difficulties, as is pointed out in paragraph 50. As the OECD Report assumes that the treaty application depends on the domestic tax treatment in State R, the question arises how State S can verify whether a person is truly entitled to the treaty benefits. The OECD Report suggests a solution that is too simple. The application of the provisions of the tax treaty between S and R should depend on whether State S is able to obtain all the necessary information. Although not expressly stated, the OECD Report obviously assumes that it is up to the taxpayer to provide State S with the necessary information. Such a result cannot be accepted. The reason why granting the tax treaty benefits in State S requires obtaining information from State R, is merely the position taken by the OECD Report that the tax treatment in State R is conditional for the application of the tax treaty between S and R. It could be shown that this opinion is not convincing. The practical difficulties arising from this position provide another argument for rejecting it.

Although the OECD Report does not deal with that question, not only withholding tax reductions in State S can be applied in that example, but also relief from double taxation is provided. As the partnership might constitute a permanent establishment for the partners A and B under the tax treaty between R and P, State R is obliged either to exempt the income attributed to the partnership or to credit the tax levied in State P. Under the tax treaty between S and R, State R has to credit the tax levied in State S. If State R has agreed to the credit method in relation to both States, the only problem might be that the tax imposed in State R might exceed the amount of tax imposed both in States P and S. In such a situation, the limitation included in Article 23 of the OECD Model Tax Convention might prevent State R from granting full relief from double taxation. If State R exempts the income attributable to the partnership in State P, a problem might arise, because due to the tax treaty between R and P, the partnership's whole income including interest income is not taxed at all in State R, except for the provison safeguarding progression. If the interest is not taxed in State R, State R is not obliged to credit any tax levied in State S. Double taxation might remain, since the tax treaty between S and P is not applicable. Of course, these problems only arise if the tax treaties concluded by State S give State S the right to levy tax on interest up to a certain percentage.

However, if this is the case, the situation could be improved if the tax treaty between R and P contained a permanent establishment non-discrimination clause. Such a clause could oblige State P to treat income arising in State S as if this income were received by an enterprise of State P. This would mean that both States R and P are obliged to credit the tax still imposed on the interest in State S after the application of the tax treaty between R and S. But this would not lead to a double exemption. Either State R exempts the income attributed to the partnership in P. Then State R would not credit the tax levied by State S either. Or State R would credit both the taxes imposed in P and S. Then one has to take into account that less tax is levied in State P because State P itself credits the tax levied in State S. Therefore, the amount of tax to be credited in State R is also reduced.

3. Example 3

P is an entity established in State P. A and B are P's partners who reside in State R. States P and S both treat P as a transparent entity but State R treats it as a taxable entity. P derives business profits from State S that are not attributable to a permanent establishment in State S.

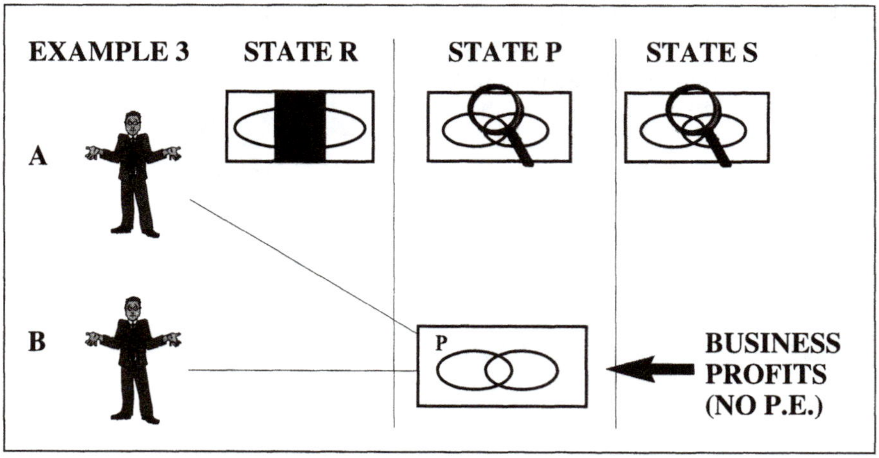

51. Here, unlike the first two examples, there is a difference in the allocation of the income involved among the countries. State S, under its domestic law treats A and B as the relevant taxpayers. However, when it comes to apply the S-R treaty, it is crucial that State R, while it generally treats A and B as residents, does not allocate to them the income arising in State S since, under the domestic law of State R, that income is allocated to P, an entity which is not resident, i.e., not liable to tax in State R. Thus in these circumstances, State S would not be required to extend the benefits of the Convention to the income which State R allocates to P for the purposes of determining the liability to State R's tax on that income, a conclusion which may be reached by a number of different routes as explained below. Correspondingly, for the purposes of applying the S-R Convention, the treatment of P in State P is not relevant, though of course it would be important in the application of the S-P Convention as will be discussed in subsequent examples.

52. The Committee views the outcome in the above examples as resulting from an application of the Convention that takes account of the basic purposes of the Convention: to eliminate double taxation and to prevent double non-taxation. As discussed in the introductory section of this Report, it recognizes that the existing Convention and Commentary do not deal explicitly with many of the issues which arise in the treatment of partnerships under the Convention. Under a literal application of the

provisions of the Convention, a partnership that is not itself liable to tax would not be entitled to the benefits of the Convention and to the extent that the income derived by or paid to the partnership would not be considered to be derived by or paid to the partners themselves, the partners would also be precluded from claiming the benefits of the Convention with respect to the partnership's income. To avoid the result that the provisions of tax Conventions do not apply to the income of a transparent partnership, it is therefore necessary to determine whether and how it would be possible to obtain the desired results under the structure of the existing Convention.

53. One broadly-based approach would be to recognize as implicit in the structure of the Convention the principle that the source State, in applying the Convention where partnerships are involved, should take into account, as part of the factual context in which the Convention is to be applied, the way in which an item of income arising in its jurisdiction is treated in the jurisdiction of the taxpayer claiming the benefits of the treaty as a resident. If that State 'flows through' the income to the partner, then the partner should be considered liable to tax and entitled to the benefits of the Convention of the State of which he is a resident. It may be observed, in that respect, that a partner is still to be considered liable to tax on the income which 'flows through' to him where, in the State of residence, tax is not imposed on that income by virtue of, e.g., a participation exemption in the case of dividends or the application of the exemption method for the relief of double taxation in the case of income attributable to a permanent establishment. On the other hand, if the income, though allocated to the taxpayer under the laws of the source State, is not similarly allocated for purposes of determining the liability to tax on that item of income in the State of residence of the taxpayer claiming the benefits of the Convention, then the source State should not grant benefits under the Convention. In these latter circumstances, the underlying factual premise on which the allocation of taxing rights is based, that is, that the source State is only obliged to reduce its domestic law tax claim where the income in question is potentially liable to tax in the hands of a resident of the treaty partner, is simply not present. This interpretation, which looks at how the partnership's income is taxed by the State of residence, avoids denying the benefits of tax Conventions to a partnership's income on the basis that neither the partnership, because it is not a resident, nor the partners, because the income is not directly paid to them or derived by them, can claim the benefits of the Convention with respect to that income.

54. Another approach would involve consideration of the terms of the distributive rules in the relevant articles of the Convention. Under that analysis, in the case of dividends, interest and royalties, the inquiry

would be whether or not the recipient of the item of income was the beneficial owner of the income under the laws of the State of residence of the taxpayer claiming treaty benefits and thus the taxpayer in relation to the income. In the case of a partnership treated as transparent under the laws of the source State but as a taxable entity under the laws of the residence State, the entity itself and not the partners would be treated as the beneficial owner. Because of the treatment of the income in the State of residence, the partners would not be the beneficial owners of the income for purposes of the treaty. Thus the partners would not be entitled to treaty benefits in those circumstances and whether the entity was so entitled would depend on whether it independently qualified as a resident. Similarly, where business profits are involved, the determination of whether the profits were attributable to an enterprise 'of' the residence State of the taxpayer claiming the benefits would be determined by the source State on the basis of the treatment of the situation in the residence State. Again, if the partnership was treated as an entity by that latter State, it, and not the partners, would be the relevant party which would be required to establish a claim for treaty benefits.

55. Finally, some countries would feel constrained to follow the allocation of the income under their principles of domestic law, even when that results in the income being subject to taxation in the State of source and taxation in the hands of the partners under the law of their State of residence. Even those countries, however, recognize the desirability of some mechanism to relieve the resulting double taxation and either provide for the situation in special provisions in their Conventions or at least show a willingness to relieve the double taxation through the mechanism of the mutual agreement procedure, particularly where a distribution of the partnership income is made in the year in which the income is realized.

56. In the light of the preceding analysis, the Committee has therefore agreed to add the following paragraph to the Commentary to Article 4:

> '8.2 Where a State disregards a partnership for tax purposes and treats it as fiscally transparent, taxing only the partners on their share of the partnership income, the partnership itself is not liable to tax and may not, therefore, be considered a resident of that State. In such a case, since the income of the partnership 'flows through' to the partners under the domestic law of that State, the partners are the persons who are liable to tax on that income and are thus the appropriate persons to claim the benefits of the Conventions concluded by the States of which they are residents. This latter result will obtain even if, under the domestic law of the State of source, the income is attributed to a partnership which is treated as a separate taxable entity. For States which could not agree with this

> interpretation of the Article, it would be possible to provide for this result in a special provision which would avoid the resulting potential double taxation where the income of the partnership is differently allocated by the two States'.

The OECD Report discusses the problem at length, which it has created itself. As pointed out, there is absolutely no need to look at the domestic tax treatment in State R. According to the domestic concept of State S, the taxpayers to whom the income of the partnership is allocated, are the partners A and B. Therefore, it would be logical to examine of which State the partners are residents. According to the example, State R is the State of residence. Consequently, the partners should be entitled to the treaty benefits in State S. It does not matter that State R does not allocate the income to the partners. Not allocating income to the partners by State R leads to the same result as exempting this income at the level of the partners. According to the prevailing opinion, the entitlement to treaty benefits does not require the imposition of taxes in the other Contracting State. Such a premise would only be correct if a tax treaty contains a 'subject-to-tax-clause'. As the OECD Model Tax Convention does not contain such a clause, it is against the object and purpose of the OECD Model Tax Convention to simulate one. Therefore, there is no reason to refuse the treaty benefits of the tax treaty between S and R in State S.

The drafters of the OECD Report are to a certain extent prisoners of their own concept. As they look at the tax treatment in State R, they conclude that, according to the domestic law of State R, the income is allocated to the partnership as such. Nevertheless, they see difficulties in granting the treaty benefits to the partnership, since the partnership was established in State P and is therefore not resident of State R. Assuming that the underlying assumption, namely looking at the treatment in State R, is correct, the conclusions are at least consistent. However, the next step is not consistent: even from the premises made by the OECD Report it should be derived that the partners A and B are entitled to the treaty benefits, as they are residents of State R. The OECD Report admits that 'a partner is still to be considered liable to tax on the income which 'flows through' to him where, in the State of residence, tax is not imposed on that income by virtue of, e.g., a participation exemption in the case of dividends or the application of the exemption method for the relief of double taxation in the case of income attributable to a permanent establishment'. But then the OECD Report makes a distinction which is not convincing at all: 'On the other hand, if the income, though allocated to the taxpayer under the laws of the source State, it is not similarily allocated for purposes of determining the liability to tax on that item of income in the State of residence of the taxpayer claiming the tax treaty benefits of the Convention, then the source State should not grant benefits under the Convention'. As just pointed out, both situations have in common that income is not taxed at the level of the partner. As far as a tax treaty does not contain a subject-to-tax provision, the entitlement to tax treaty benefits must not depend on the imposition of tax in the other Contracting State. The OECD Report takes the wrong premises and therefore draws the wrong conclusions. As the 'basic purpose' of the OECD Model Tax Convention is not 'to prevent double non-taxation', there is no justification to simulate the existence of a 'subject-to-tax-clause'. Treaty benefits have to be granted irrespective of whether the other Contracting State exercises its taxing rights or not as provided by the tax treaty.

The other approach mentioned in the OECD Report, namely looking at the wording of the distributive rules of the OECD Model Tax Convention is not convincing either. It does not make sense to focus on the fact that in the case of dividends, interest and royalties, the OECD Model Tax Convention has used the phrase 'beneficial owner', at least since 1977. According to the alternative approach contained in the OECD Report, the recipient of dividends, interest and royalties has to be the beneficial owner, if the tax treaty benefits should be granted. Then, the OECD Report argues that only the taxpayer to whom the income is allocated according the domestic law of the State of residence, may qualify as 'beneficial owner'. If this assumption were correct, one would have to conclude that there is a major distinction between those distributive rules which contain the phrase 'beneficial owner' and those which do not. However, the OECD Report does not indicate how partnerships with other types of income, such as income from immovable property, should be treated. The drafters of the OECD Report only touch on the case of business profits and suggest that the phrase 'enterprise of a Contracting State' should be understood in a way that the tax treatment in the residence State should be conditional for the entitlement to tax treaty benefits in the source State. However, as already pointed out, such an interpretation does not indicate how partnerships with other types of income should be treated. Furthermore, it is not convincing why the term 'enterprise of a Contracting State' should be read as a 'subject-to-tax-clause', since this term means, according to Article 3 paragraph 1 subparagraph (c) of the OECD Model Tax Convention, 'an enterprise carried on by a resident of a Contracting State'. This definition does not mention that this resident should not only be liable to tax but also be effectively taxed. Similarily, the term 'beneficial owner' does not indicate that only those residents should qualify who effectively have to bear the tax burden in the State of residence. In summary, it does neither seem convincing that there should be a major distinction between certain distributive rules and others, some containing a 'subject-to-tax-clause', some not, nor is it persuasive that the terms 'beneficial owner' and 'enterprise of a Contracting State' should be read as a 'subject-to-tax-clause'.

The OECD Report takes the premise that there is no double taxation in such a situation and that it is therefore not necessary to apply the tax treaties. Even this premise can be challenged. Although it is true that there is no tax imposed in State R, both State S and State P impose taxes on the business profits. Both States S and P apply a look-through approach and allocate the income to the partners. Since the partners are neither residents of State S nor of State P, the tax treaty between S and P cannot be applied. However, if the partnership constitutes a permanent establishment in State P under the tax treaty between R and P and the tax treaty between R and P contains a permanent establishment non-discrimination clause, one might conclude that State P has to treat A and B with their permanent establishment in State P in the same way State P would treat an enterprise of State P. Therefore, State P could be obliged to credit the same amount of tax imposed in State S against the tax levied in State P as it would in the case of an enterprise of State P. This could lead at least to a partial relief from double taxation. However, any withholding tax reduction that the tax treaty between S and P would provide, of course, cannot be applied, since the non-discrimination clause of the tax treaty between R and P cannot create an obligation for a third State. On the other hand, only the amount of tax may be credited, State P would have to credit against its own taxes if the tax treaty between P and S were applicable. This means that State P would credit only the amount of tax State S would be allowed to levy according to the tax treaty, although the withholding tax reduction as such is not applicable. If the tax treaty is similar to the OECD Model Tax Convention, State S would not be allowed to levy any tax on business profits as there is no permanent establishment in State S. Double taxation therefore remains.

However, one has to keep in mind that also the Commentary to the Model Tax Convention was changed. As already pointed out, changes and amendments to the Commentary are only of relevance for tax treaties concluded after the change of the OECD Commentary. Furthermore, the Commentary is not the only source of interpretation for such treaties, for whose interpretation they are at all relevant. If one focuses on the system of the OECD Model Tax Convention as such, nothing indicates that it would be of relevance for the entitlement to treaty benefits concerning how the partnership is treated in the State of residence and if the partner is liable to tax 'on the income'. Therefore, it is not convincing to interpret future tax treaties as suggested by the Commentary.

4. Example 4

P is a partnership established in State P. A and B are P's partners who reside in State P. State P treats P as a transparent entity while State S treats it as a taxable entity. P derives royalty income from State S that is not attributable to a permanent establishment in State S.

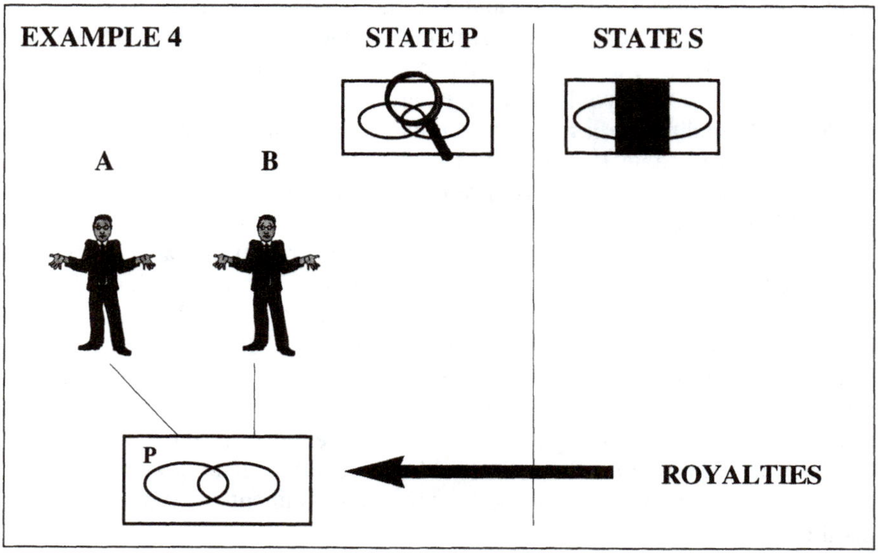

59. This example involves the fundamental difference in the tax treatment of partnerships that has already been referred to in paragraph 19 onwards above. The question is how the State S should apply the provisions of the Convention in such a case.

60. Under State S domestic law, the taxpayer will be partnership P. State S could then argue that since partnership P is not entitled to the benefits of the treaty, it can tax the income derived by P regardless of the provisions of the S-P Convention. This, however, would mean that the income on which A and B are liable to tax in State P would be subjected to tax in State S regardless of the Convention, a result that seems in direct conflict with the object and purpose of the Convention.

61. The Committee compared that approach, under which State S applies the provisions of the Convention by reference to the treatment of the partnership under its domestic law, with another approach, under which State S considers the entitlement to treaty benefits of A and B, both residents of State P, under the principles put forward above. Under the latter approach, State S would determine that the provisions of the Convention should be applied to prevent it from taxing the royalties

since, under these principles, the income must be considered to be paid to A and B, two residents of State P, who should also be considered to be the beneficial owners of such income as these are the persons liable to tax on such income in State P. The Committee concluded that this approach was the correct one as it is more likely to ensure that the benefits of the Convention accrue to the persons who are liable to tax on the income.

62. The Committee did not consider this approach to be inconsistent with the provisions of paragraph 2 of Article 3, under which terms not defined in the Convention have, unless the context provides otherwise, the meaning which they have under the domestic law of the Contracting State that applies the Convention. In the example, the tax treatment of the partnership in State P is part of the facts on the basis of which the terms of the Convention are to be applied. Thus, by referring to that tax treatment, State S does not adopt a particular interpretation of the terms of the Convention put forward by State P; it merely takes into account the facts required for the application of these terms. The Committee concluded that, in any event, if an interpretation based on domestic law would lead to cases where the income taxed in the hands of residents of one State would not get the benefits of the Convention, a result that would be contrary to the object and purpose of the Convention, the context of the Convention would require a different interpretation.

Again, the OECD Report prefers a certain interpretation because 'it is more likely to ensure that the benefits of the Convention accrue to the persons who are liable to tax on the income'. The drafters of the OECD Report ignore that, according to Article 4 OECD Model Tax Convention, it is not relevant if a person is 'liable to tax on the income', but it is sufficient if a person is merely 'liable to tax'.

Furthermore, the OECD Report gives the impression that the drafters compared two different approaches and finally preferred the one more favourable to the taxpayer. They assume that the approach, under which State S applies the provisions of the Convention by reference to the treatment of the partnership under its domestic law, leads to the result that the tax treaty is not at all applicable. However, this assumption has to be challenged, as the partnership is, according to the domestic law of State S, treated as a taxable entity. If its seat or place of management is in State P, there is a very good argument that the tax treaty between S and P is applicable. Therefore, the approach rejected by the OECD Report is not the less favourable one, but the more favourable, if one follows the solution suggested here.

In the light of these deliberations, there is no need to make reference to Article 3 paragraph 2 of the OECD Model Tax Convention. The OECD Report refers to Article 3 paragraph 2 of the OECD Model Tax Convention to justify an approach which seems to be more favourable to the taxpayer.

Since this assumption is not correct, Article 3 paragraph 2 of the OECD Model Tax Convention is not required to arrive at an interpretation which is in accordance with the object and the purpose of the treaty. It is sufficient to look at the taxpayer to whom the income is allocated in the source State, as this taxpayer, namely the partnership, easily qualifies as a resident person.

It is another question whether there is relief from double taxation in a situation described in this example. The OECD Report does not deal with that issue. As the Contracting States allocate the income to different taxpayers, namely to the partnership in State S and to the partners in State P, there seems to be no relief. Tax imposed on the partnership cannot be credited against tax imposed on the partners, if withholding taxes may be levied at all. The OECD Report does not indicate that any relief from double taxation can be provided in such a situation. However, in a later example there is a remark showing that even in such a situation a tax credit is not completely unthinkable.[80]

[80] OECD, supra note 1, para 139.

5. Example 5

The facts are the same as in Example 4 above but the tax treatment of the partnership in State P and S is reversed. P is a partnership established in State P. A and B are P's partners who reside in State P. State P treats P as a taxable entity while State S treats it as a transparent entity. P derives royalty income from State S that is not attributable to a permanent establishment in State S.

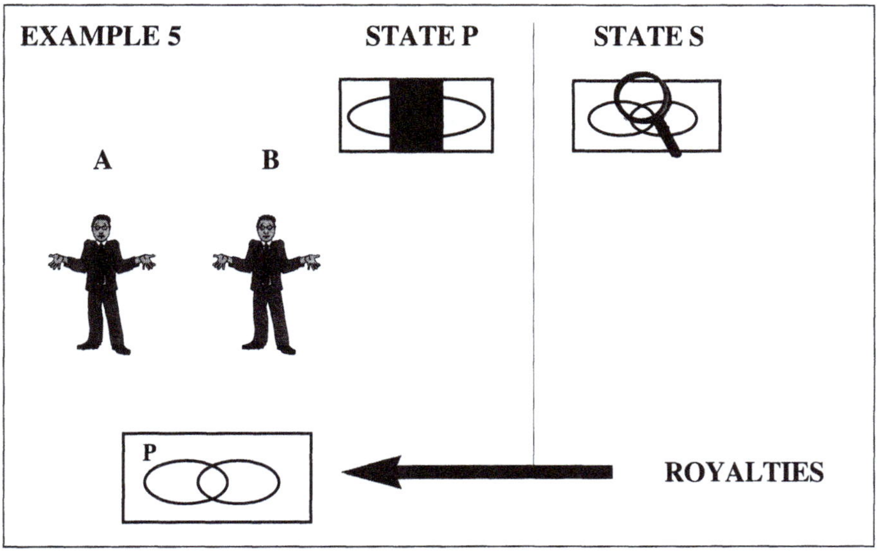

63. In this situation, in following its domestic law rules for allocating the income of the partnership, State S would treat A and B as the relevant taxpayers. However, in applying the treaty, the principles developed in Section II.4 above would require that it take into consideration that State P had allocated the income of the partnership to P. Thus, for purposes of the Convention, P would be the taxpayer entitled to claim the benefits of the Convention since it is liable to tax in State P on the income of the partnership. While, in the particular circumstances of this example, it does not make a difference whether State S considers the treaty entitlements of the partners or of the partnership, this would matter, as shown in subsequent examples, if the partner, or one of them, were not residents of State P.

Again, the OECD Report takes the premise that it is the partnership that is entitled to the treaty benefits as the partnership is treated as a taxable entity in State P. Assuming that the partners A and B might claim the treaty benefits, this would not lead to a different result, unless, as the OECD Report correctly points out, the partners are not residents of the third State.

However, although the OECD Report does not deal with that question, there seems to be no relief from double taxation in the end, if State S may levy withholding tax on royalties, according to the tax treaty. The withholding tax, levied on behalf of the partners A and B, according to the domestic law of State S, probably cannot be credited against the tax imposed on the partnership in State P, at least according to the tax treaty between P and S. Therefore, double taxation remains, if State S imposes withholding tax and State P also imposes taxation, although not at the partners but at the level of the partnership. However, another paragraph of this Report indicates that a credit seems possible.[81]

[81] OECD, supra note 1, para 139.

6. Example 6

P is a partnership established in State P. A and B are P's partners who reside in State R. State P treats P as a transparent entity while State R treats it as a taxable entity. P derives royalty income from State P that is not attributable to a permanent establishment in that State.

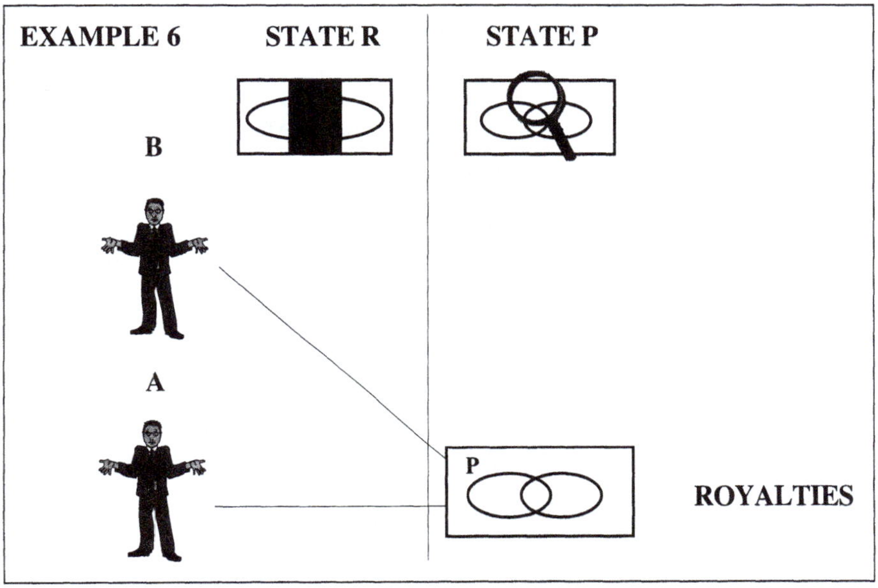

64. While the Committee agrees that in this situation State P should not be required to give the benefits of the Convention with respect to the royalty income, several different approaches are used to support this result. Using one approach, partners A and B, though residents as such of State R are not liable to tax on the partnership income under the allocation rules applied by State R, consequently they are not entitled to benefits under the Convention in respect of that income. P is not a resident of State R for purposes of the Convention since, from the perspective of State R, it is not a domestic taxpayer in any sense. Thus again, State P's right to tax the partnership income would not be restricted under the Convention.

65. Alternatively, as discussed in paragraph 54 above, the partners would not be entitled to benefits under the Convention because they would not be considered as beneficial owners of the income for purposes of the Convention. Adopting a more literal approach, State P might simply focus on the fact that, under its allocation rules, the income has been paid to P and P would not qualify as a resident either of State R or State P. Here the treatment of A and B would not be relevant.

66. Finally, some countries would deny treaty benefits to A and B based on concepts of bad faith or abuse of treaty rights. The distributive rules of the Convention are based on the underlying assumption that A and B would be attributed the income on which treaty relief would be granted and where that is not the case, these general concepts would allow State P to resist any claims by A or B for benefits.

The OECD Report starts its deliberation by reporting the result: the Committee agrees that in this situation State P should not be required to give the benefits of the Convention with respect to the royalty income. It seems that just as a second step the Committee looks for arguments supporting this result. This impression is not completely satisfactory.

The first approach to support this result mentioned in the OECD Report is not convincing: the OECD Report ignores that A and B are 'liable to tax' in State R and therefore entitled to the treaty benefits. The taxation of a certain type of income is no requirement for the entitlement to the treaty benefits in respect to this income, as the OECD Model Tax Convention does not contain a general 'subject-to-tax-clause'. As already pointed out, the term 'beneficial ownership' contained in Articles 10, 11 and 12 of the OECD Model Tax Convention does not constitute a 'subject-to-tax-clause' either.

The approach described as 'more literal' is not convincing either. The OECD Report suggests that 'State P might simply focus on the fact that, under its allocation rules, the income has been paid to P and P would not qualify as a resident either of State R or State P'. Although it is true that P does not qualify as a resident either of State R and State P, however it is not correct that under the allocation rules of State P the income has been paid to P. According to the facts given in Example 6 above, State P does not treat the partnership as a taxable entity but applies a look-through approach. Therefore, State P does allocate the income to the partners.

The final approach described in the Report is even less convincing. It has to be noted that even the OECD Report seems to disassociate itself from this opinion, as it emphasises that 'some countries' would apply this approach. There is no reason why the entitlement to the treaty benefits should be refused in Example 6 above 'on concepts of bad faith or abuse of treaty rights'. It is not the taxpayer's fault that the Contracting States domestically treat the partnership differently. Therefore, there is no justification for a denial of treaty benefits due to 'bad faith' or 'abuse of law'. Furthermore, it is hotly debated whether treaty benefits could under any circumstances be denied due to domestic anti-abuse provisions, as domestic law and tax treaty law have to be kept separate for interpretation purposes.[82] Again, the Committee admits that it

[82] Debatin, 'Qualifikationsprobleme im Doppelbesteuerungsrecht' (1979) *FR*, p. 493 (p. 493); Gassner and M. Lang, in Gassner, M. Lang and Lechner (eds), *Entwicklungen*, p. 58; Gröhs and Herbst, (1986) *ZfV*, p. 25; M. Lang, 'Die Auslegung von Doppelbesteuerungsabkommen' (1993) *CDFI* LXXVIIIa, p. 197 (pp. 199 et seq.).

assumes that 'the distributive rules of the Convention are based on the underlying assumption that A and B would be attributed the income on which treaty relief would be granted and where that is not the case, these general concepts would allow State P to resist any claims by A and B for benefits'. As it has been repeatedly pointed out, it is questionable if such an 'underlying assumption' can be based on the OECD Model Tax Convention.

However, surprisingly the OECD Report does not give another reasoning to support the result the Committee is in favour of. Accepting that A and B are entitled to treaty benefits, does not necessarily mean that the withholding tax reduction for royalties under the tax treaty between R and P is applicable. If the partnership constitutes a permanent establishment for the partners A and B in State P, the royalty income has to be attributed to this permanent establishment. If this is the case, according to Article 12 paragraph 3 of the OECD Model Tax Convention the withholding tax reduction for royalties is not applicable: 'The provisions of paragraph 1 shall not apply if the beneficial owner of the royalties, being a resident of a Contracting State, carries on business in the other Contracting State in which the royalties arise, through a permanent establishment situated therein, and the right or property in respect of which the royalties are paid is effectly connected with such permanent establishment or fixed base. In such case the provision of Article 7 or Article 14, as the case may be, shall apply'. According to Article 7, State P has the right to tax. At the level of the partners A and B State R has either to exempt the income or to credit the tax imposed in State P, which is meaningless, as State R does not levy any tax at the level of the partners A and B. However, State P is not prevented from taxing the royalties at whatever rate is provided in its domestic law.

Irrespective of the approach one follows, there is relief from double taxation in a situation described in Example 6 above. However, this is not due to the tax treaty but to the domestic law of State R: as State R does not allocate the income to the partners A and B, but to the partnership and the partnership is not resident of State R, State R does not exercise its taxing rights provided in the treaty.

7. Example 7

68. Triangular cases pose difficult problems with respect to the determination of entitlement to treaty benefits. The Committee believes, however, that these problems may be solved through the application of the same principles put forward in paragraphs 52 and 53 above. The following examples discuss how these principles should be applied in different situations involving three States.

P is a partnership established in State P. A and B are P's partners who reside in State R. P owns shares in X, a company that is a resident of State S. X pays a dividend to P. State R and S treat P as a taxable entity while State P treats it as fiscally transparent.

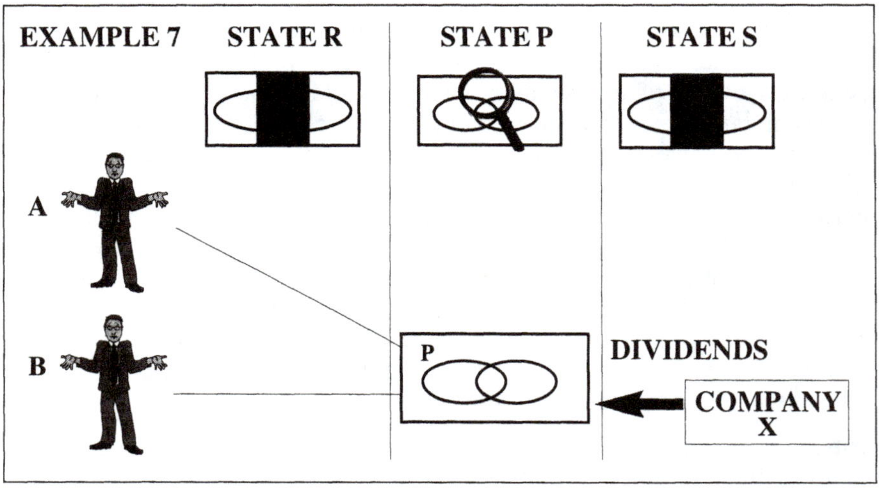

69. In this situation, the partnership it not liable to tax in State P and is therefore not a resident of that State for purposes of the P-S Convention. Similarly, though P is treated as the taxpayer for purposes of the domestic law of State S and the income is allocated to P under the domestic laws of R, P is not liable to tax in State R because it is not treated as a resident. Finally, though A and B are potentially liable to tax as residents in State R, under R's allocation rules, the income is not allocated to them but to P. Thus P is not a resident of State R and A and B are not entitled to benefit from the R-S Convention with respect to the partnership's income. State S would thus be entitled to tax the income without restriction.

70. It should be noted that, in this example (as in the following examples), the tax treatment of partnerships in State S does not have any impact on

the entitlement to treaty benefits. Thus, the S-R and S-P Conventions would still not be applicable with respect to the dividends if State S treated partnerships as transparent rather that taxable entities.

The OECD Report arrives at a solution where no relief from double taxation is provided. According to the OECD Report, State S can mantain its withholding tax. Neither the tax treaty between S and P nor the tax treaty between S and R were applicable. This result is the consequence of the premises taken by the Committee. The members of the Commitee consider how the recipient of the income is treated in the other Contracting State. According to the domestic law of State P, the income is allocated to the partners A and B. As they are not residents of P, the tax treaty between P and S cannot be applied. According to the domestic law of State R, the income is allocated to the partnership. Although the partnership is treated as a taxable entity, it is not resident of State R. Therefore, the Committee concludes that the benefits granted by the tax treaty between R and S have to be denied.

Again, the OECD Report ignores that A and B are 'liable to tax' according to the domestic law of State R. Although the income is not allocated to them by the domestic law of State R, they are residents of R. If the OECD Report adhered to its own premises, there would be no reason to deny the treaty benefits to A and B. The taxation of a certain income in the hands of the partners is no requirement for their entitlement to the treaty benefits. The OECD Report reads into the treaty a non-existing 'subject-to-tax-clause'.

The OECD Report explicitly emphasises that the tax treatment of partnerships in State S does not have any impact on the entitlement to treaty benefits. It is deplorable that no reason is given why that position has been taken. On the contrary, as already pointed out, it would be very convincing to look at the tax treatment in State S. Since State S treats the partnership as a taxable entity, it would be consistent to examine whether the partnership is entitled to the treaty benefits. This question can be answered affirmatively. The partnership is established in State P and therefore fulfills the criteria necessary to be treated as a resident. According to the approach suggested here, the treaty between S and P is applicable.

The OECD Report does not examine if the tax treaties in question provide for relief from double taxation. In the situation described in Example 7 above, State R does not impose any tax either on the partnership or on the partners A and B. However, States P and S impose taxes. State P applies a look-through approach and might therefore assume that the partnership established in State P constitutes a permanent establishment for the partners A and B and therefore levy tax. State S might levy a withholding tax, according to the approach followed by the OECD Report, even without any restriction. Since on the one hand State P does not allocate the income to the partnership as such, and, on the other hand, the withholding tax in State S is levied on behalf of the partnership, this withholding tax cannot be credited in State P. Even the application of a non-discrimination clause contained in the tax treaty between P and R cannot provide for relief from double taxation. The non-discrimination-clause could lead to the application of the tax treaty between State S and State P, however, that still does not help, if the income is allocated to different taxpayers in these two States.

8. Example 8

The facts are the same as in Example 7 above except that the tax treatment of the partnership in State P is reversed. P is a partnership established in State P. A and B are P's partners who reside in State R. P owns shares in X, a company that is a resident of State S. X pays a dividend to P. All States treat P as a taxable entity.

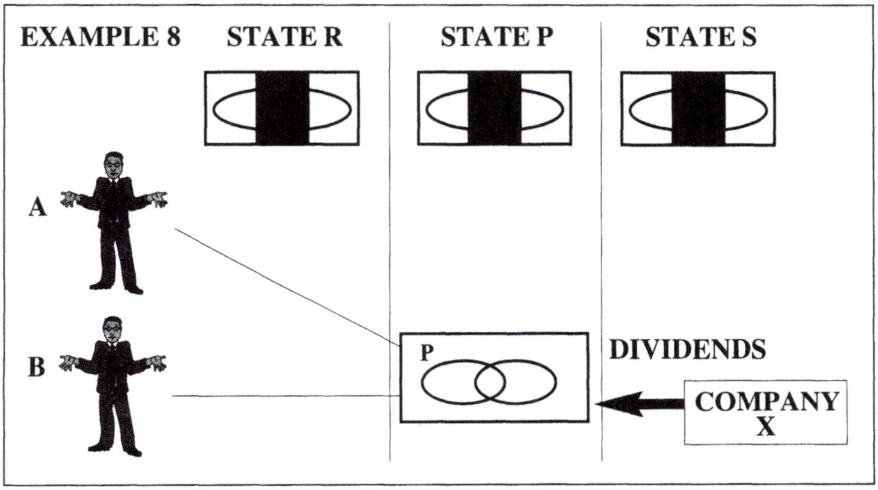

71. In this example, partnership P is a resident of State P as it is liable to tax therein. Partners A and B should not be considered to be entitled to the benefits of the S-R Convention with respect to the partnership income as they are not liable to tax on that income. Conversely, P should be considered by State S to be entitled to the benefits of the S-P Convention in relation to the dividends it derives from that State as it is liable to tax on those dividends and should therefore be considered to be the recipient and beneficial owner of that income. Thus the S-P Convention will restrict State S' right to tax the dividends, even if State S taxes the dividends in the hands of partners A and B under its domestic rules applicable to the taxation of partnerships. It should be noted, however, that since P is a partnership, it will not get the benefits of the reduced rate of tax provided for in subparagraph 2(a) of Article 10 of the Model Tax Convention (the subparagraph expressly excludes partnerships from its application) unless the two Contracting States agree to modify subparagraph 2(a) to give the benefits of the reduced rate to a partnership treated as a body corporate (compare paragraph 11 of the Commentary on Article 10).

72. As already mentioned, the tax treatment of partnerships in State S does not have any impact on the entitlement to treaty benefits in this case. Thus, the S-P Convention would still be the only relevant one if State S treated partnerships as transparent rather than taxable entities.

Again, this example shows that the OECD Report exclusively looks at the tax treatment of the recipient of the income in his home State. It is explicitly mentioned that the tax treatment of partnerships in State S does not have any impact on the entitlement to treaty benefits in this case. As already pointed out in the discussion of another example, this approach seems to be inconsistent, as the Committee ignores that the partners A and B are also residents of a Contracting State, namely State R, and should therefore also be entitled to the treaty benefits if one really looks at the tax treatment in the other Contracting State, and not in the source State.

However, if one nevertheless focuses on the person to whom the income is allocated in the source State, this inconsistency can be avoided. As State S treats the partnership as a taxable entity and the partnership has been established in State P, one should therefore conclude that the tax treaty between S and P is applicable, if the partnership has its seat or place of management in P. On the contrary, the tax treaty between S and R is not applicable, as the partnership cannot be considered a resident of R: although it is a taxable entity according to the domestic treatment in State S, it does not have the necessary links (close ties) to State R.

Although not discussed by the OECD Report, relief from double taxation is provided to a certain extent. As State P treats the partnership as a taxable entity, State P is obliged to credit the tax levied in State S on behalf of the partnership. State R probably taxes the income of the partners. As State P treats the partnership as a taxable entity, the partners receive dividend income according to Article 10 of the OECD Model Tax Convention. As Article 10 paragraph 3 of the OECD Model Tax Convention refers to the qualification in the source State for treaty purposes,[8] this qualification is also relevant for State R as far as tax treaty purposes are concerned. If State P levies any withholding tax on the dividends, State R has to credit this withholding tax against the taxes imposed at the level of the partners in State R, as long as the amount of the withholding tax is in accordance with the tax treaty. Although, finally, tax is imposed both on the partnership and the partners, this result is not inconsistent, as this situation has to be compared with a situation where in State P a corporation is involved instead of a partnership. As far as corporations are concerned, the tax treaties as such cannot prevent an 'economic' double taxation of income in the hands of the corporation and the shareholders, since many States apply such a 'classical' system domestically.

---

[83] Vogel, *Double Taxation Conventions* (1997) Art 10 supra m.no. 186.

The situation is comparable if the partnership is treated as a taxable entity, as this is the case in Example 8 above. Therefore, this solution seems to be in accordance with the object and purpose of the treaty.

The OECD Report deals with another question, namely the interpretation of Article 10 paragraph 2 subparagraph (a) of the OECD Model Tax Convention. Without giving any reasoning, the OECD Report states that the reduced rate provided for in this provision cannot be applied, 'since P is a partnership'. Although it is correct that Article 10 paragraph 2 subparagraph (a) explicitly excludes 'partnerships' from the benefits of the reduced withholding tax rate, it is not at all clear what the term 'partnership' means in the context of this provision. The OECD Report obviously follows the approach that the term 'partnership' refers to civil law, although failing to mention which country's civil law qualification is relevant. Another approach would be to understand the 'partnership' as a transparent entity according to the qualification of the State where the partnership was established. This question deserves a thorough examination. As the Committee obviously did not have enough time to conduct such an examination, it is deplorable that it did not hesitate to give an opinion on this question. Without any reasonings given for this position, such a statement is not very helpful. Practice and national courts will probably only follow a position taken in the OECD Report if its reasoning is convincing.

9. Example 9

The facts are the same as in Example 8 above except that the tax treatment of the partnership in State R is reversed. P is a partnership established in State P. A and B are P's partners who reside in State R. P owns shares in X, a company that is a resident of State S. X pays a dividend to P. State P and State S treat P as a taxable entity while State R treats it as fiscally transparent.

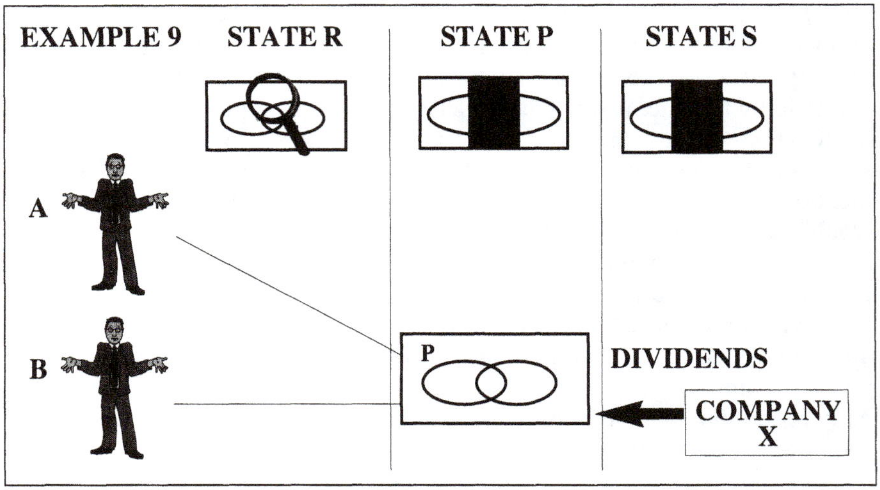

73. This example presents a case where there will be a double entitlement to treaty benefits with respect to the same income. As in the previous example, partnership P is a resident of State P as it is liable to tax therein. P should again be considered by State S to be entitled to the benefits of the S-P Convention in relation to the dividends it derives from that State as it is liable to tax on those dividends and should therefore be considered to be the recipient and beneficial owner of that income. In contrast to the previous example, however, partners A and B should also be considered to be entitled to the benefits of the S-R Convention with respect to the partnership income as they are also liable to tax on that income. Thus both the S-P and S-R Conventions will restrict State S' right to tax the dividends, regardless of whether State S taxes these dividends in the hands of the partnership or of partners A and B (under its domestic rules applicable to the taxation of partnerships, it is likely to tax them in the hands of the partnership). Again, the tax treatment of partnerships in State S has no impact on this result with the result that both Conventions would still be applicable if State S will not have any impact on this result so that both Conventions would still be applicable if State S treated partnerships as transparent rather than taxable entities.

74. The Committee agreed that this double entitlement to treaty benefits will be satisfied by State S imposing the lowest amount of tax allowed under the two treaties. Thus, if the S-R Convention restricts to 15 per cent of the

gross amount of the dividends the tax that can be levied by State S while the S-P treaty restricts the tax of 10 per cent of that amount, the obligations imposed on State S under both Conventions will be satisfied if the tax imposed by State S does not exceed 10 per cent of the dividends.

75. While the Committee agreed on that approach, it recognized the administrative difficulties that its implementation would generate in the case of a partnership which could have a large number of partners who were residents of different States.

The OECD Report comes to the conclusion that in a situation described in Example 9 above entitlement to both tax treaties, namely the tax treaty between S and P and the tax treaty between S and R, is provided. From the position taken in the OECD Report it is consistent that State S must impose the lowest amount of tax allowed under the two treaties. At the same time, the OECD Report admits that the implementation of this approach generates administrative difficulties, if the partnership has a large number of partners who are residents of different States.

These administrative difficulties can be avoided if one focuses on the tax treatment of the partnership in State S. As State S treats the partnership as a taxable entity, it is the partnership to whom the dividends are allocated. As the partnership is established in State P, it has to be considered as a resident. Therefore the partnership is entitled to the tax treaty benefits in S that the tax treaty between S and P provides for. On the other hand, the tax treaty between S and R is not applicable, since State S does not allocate the income to the partners A and B and the partnership, to whom the income is allocated, cannot be considered a resident of State R.

However, again the OECD Report does not deal with the question concerning whether relief from double taxation is provided for; State S may levy tax on the dividends up to a certain amount. This tax has to be credited in State P, as the tax levied in State S is levied on behalf of the partnership and State P treats the partnership as a taxable entity. Any 'distributions' of the partnership might be taxed in State P as dividends according to the tax treaty between P and R. State R applies a look-through approach and allocates the income of the partnership to the partners. If Article 7 of the OECD Model Tax Convention were applicable, State R would not have any taxing rights, unless the credit method provides for such types of income. However, Article 10 of the OECD Model Tax Convention is also applicable, since State P treats the partnership as a taxable entity and Article 10 paragraph 3 makes reference to the domestic law of the source State. As Article 10 of the OECD Model Tax Convention has predominance over Article 7 of the OECD Model Tax Convention,[84] Article 10 is applicable. This means that State R may impose tax on the partners and, at the same time has to credit any withholding tax levied on these dividends in State P.

[84] M. Lang, *Finanzierungen*, p. 81; M. Lang, in Kleineidam (ed.), *FS Lutz Fischer* (1999) pp. 720 et seq.; OECD, MC Commentary, Art 7 supra m.no. 34 et seq.

10. Example 10

The facts are the same as in Example 9 above except that there is no tax Convention between States S and P.

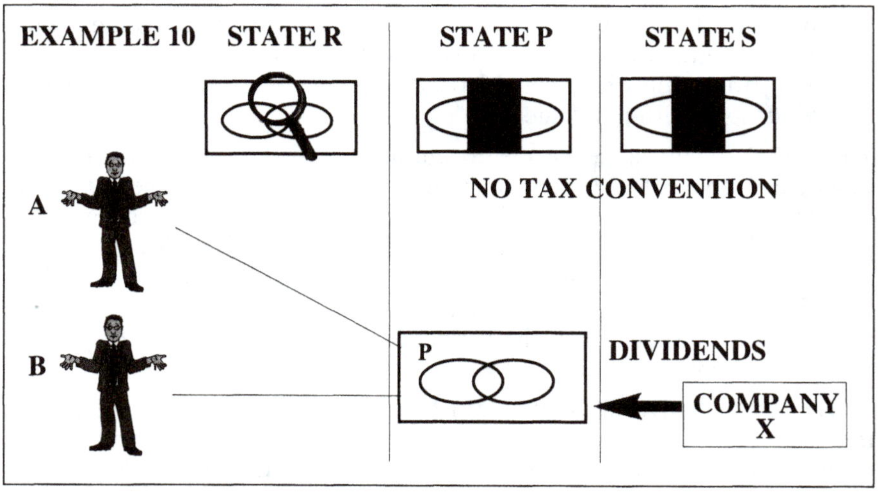

76. The Committee also discussed how the principles and conclusions formulated in its analysis of the previous examples would apply if the partnership were a resident of a State with which the State of source did not have a tax Convention, including the case where the partnership was a resident of a tax haven. It concluded that same conclusions should apply as concerns the application of the Convention between the State of source and the State of residence of the partners.
77. Thus, in this example, partners A and B should be considered to be entitled to the benefits of the S-R Convention in respect of the dividends as they are both taxable in State R on these dividends.
78. As already noted, States should not, however, be expected to grant the benefits of a tax Convention in cases where they cannot verify whether a person is truly entitled to these benefits. Thus if State P is a tax haven from which State S cannot obtain tax information, the application of the provisions of the S-R Convention will be conditional on State S being able to obtain all the necessary information from the partners or from State R. In such cases, State S might well decide to use the refund mechanism for the purposes of applying the limitation of tax provided for in Article 10 even though it normally applies this limitation at the time of the payment.

The only difference between Example 9 above and Example 10 above is the fact that there is no tax treaty between S and P. According to the approach suggested here, the absence of a tax treaty between S and P leads to the result that there is no tax treaty providing for a reduction of withholding tax in State S. However, the OECD Report takes the position that the tax treaty between S and R is applicable and provides for such a reduction.

Surprisingly, when discussing this example, the OECD Report emphasises that 'the application of the provisions of the S-R Convention will be conditional on State S being able to obtain all necessary information from the partners or State R'. First, one wonders why this problem is dealt with in the context of this example. If these questions were relevant for the entitlement to treaty benefits, this would be also true in the other situations described in the OECD Report. The major difference between Example 10 above and other examples is that no tax Convention had been concluded between two States, namely S and P. However, it is not clear why the lack of a tax treaty between P and S should have any impact on the application of the tax treaty between S and R. State P can never be held responsible to provide information necessary for the application of the tax treaty between S and R, irrespective of whether or not State P is referred to as a tax haven. Secondly, it is surprising that the OECD Report deals with the information issue at all. Although information is necessary for the application of tax treaties, it depends on the domestic law whether the taxpayer or the tax authorities have to provide this information. However, there is no tax treaty rule saying that the application of a tax treaty may be refused if no information can be obtained. If, for example, it is the obligation of the tax authorities to establish all the facts according to a specific domestic law, it cannot be to the disadvantage of the taxpayer if the tax authorities do not succeed. The OECD Report simulates a provision that does not exist in the OECD Model Tax Convention.

11. Example 11

79. As indicated in paragraph 21 above, differences in how States apply the transparency approach may create difficulties in the application of tax Conventions. Where a State considers that a partnership does not qualify as a resident because it is not liable to tax and the partners are liable to tax in their State of residence on their share of the partnership's income, it is expected that that State will apply the provisions of the Convention as if the partners had earned the income directly so that the classification of the income for purposes of the allocative rules of Articles 6 to 21 will not be modified by the fact that the income flows-through the partnership.

80. Difficulties may arise, however, in the application of provisions which refer to the activities of the taxpayer, the nature of the taxpayer, the relationship between the taxpayer and another party to a transaction. States may have different views as to what extent the partnership should be ignored in applying such rules. The following subsections describe how the Committee believes that some of the provisions of the Convention should be applied in that respect.

Company A carries on a business of engineering and company B carries on a business of electrical installation. Both companies are residents of State P. They have established a partnership P in State P for the purpose of a contract to design and install the electrical equipment in a nuclear reactor being built in State S. As part of the obligations of P under the contract, employees of Company A will be present on the construction site from 1 January to 10 June and employees of Company B will be there from 10 June to 1 February. When performing their duties, these employees will act as employees of the respective companies, each company acting as agent for the partnership.

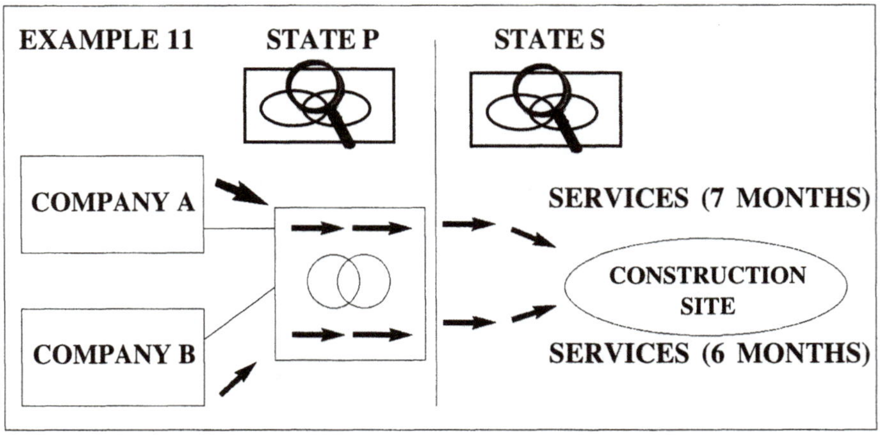

81. In this example, the Committee concluded that the period of time spent by the two partners should be aggregated at the partnership level with the result that the 12 month limit of paragraph 3 of Article 5 is exceeded. The enterprise carried on by the partnership will therefore be considered to have a permanent establishment in State S so that each partner will be considered to have a permanent establishment in State S for the purposes of the taxation of their share of the business profits derived by the partnership from State S. This conclusion would not hold good if the relationship between A and B constituted merely a joint venture or consortium as opposed to a partnership.

The OECD Report also discusses some specific problems, which arise in respect of partnerships. Although in these situations it is not the entitlement to treaty benefits that is at stake, but the application of the distributive rules of the OECD Model Tax Convention. Discussing Example 11 above, the OECD Report concludes that the period of time spent by the two partners should be aggregated at the partnership level. This seems to be a reasonable approach, although the other possible solution, namely not aggregating the period of time, seems reasonable as well. The OECD Report does not contain the reasons why the first approach is preferred. This is deplorable because the solution argued by the OECD Report would have been more easily followed, if the reasonings behind it were convincing.

12. Example 12

Partnership P, which has been established in State P, has a fixed base in State R. Partner A is a resident of State P and Partner B is a resident of State R. They have agreed to divide the profits of the partnership equally. P earns 1,500,000 during the taxable period. 1,000,000 of that amount is attributable to the services performed by B from the State R fixed base. The remaining 500,000 is attributable to services performed by A in State P. Both States treat partnerships as transparent entities.

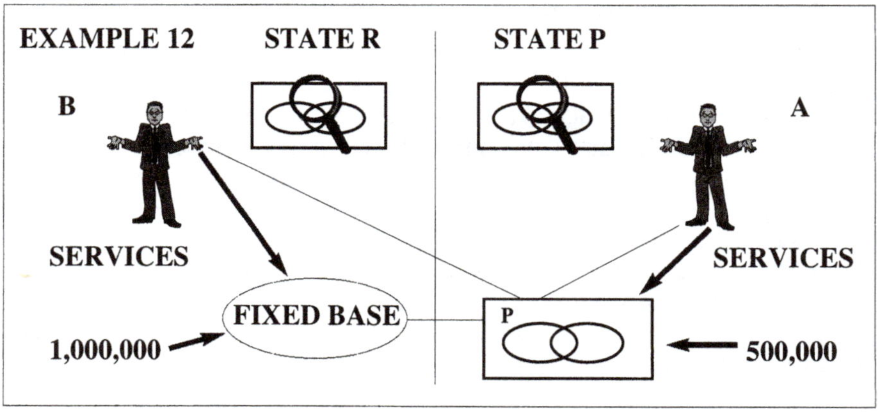

82. This example raises the question of the extent to which a transparent partnership should be ignored for the purposes of the application of Article 7 and 14. The Committee agreed that under Article 14, P's fixed base in State R should be considered to be a fixed base of both A and B and that the same is true for a permanent establishment under Article 7.

83. The Committee then considered to what extent the activities of the partnership could be similarly allocated to each of the partners for the purposes of applying paragraph 1 of Article 14, which requires that the fixed base be regularly available to a person 'for the purpose of performing his activities'.

84. Two views were expressed. Under the first view, the reference to 'his activities' in paragraph 1 of Article 14 refers to the personal activities of each partner and the partnership's activities cannot be flowed-through to the partner. According to that view, Article 14 would not allow State R to tax partner A on his share of the income attributable to the fixed base (500,000) since the fixed base was not regularly available to A for the purposes of his own personal activities.

85. The majority, however, agreed with the different view that the activities of the partnership should be allocated to the partners to the same extent that the fixed base of the partnership is attributed to each of them.

Applying this approach to the above example, State R would be allowed, as a source State, to tax partners A and partner B on their respective share of the income attributable to the fixed base located therein. State R will also be allowed, as the residence State, to tax partner B's share of any other partnership income. Similarly, State P will be allowed, as a source State, to tax all the partnership's income attributable to the fixed base of the partnership that is located in that State.

86. The Committee realised, however, that cases in the real world are rarely as simple as this example. The partnership agreement may specifically allocate the income from various States to particular partners. Entities that may be considered as partnerships for some purposes may not be partnerships for tax purposes; many international partnerships grant considerable autonomy, both managerial and financial, to their in-country subsidiary organizations. Both taxpayers and tax authorities strive to avoid administratively unmanageable results.

87. The Committee decided that these issues would more appropriately be dealt with in the context of its work on issues related to Article 14. It noted, however, that there should not be differences in result whether Article 7 or Article 14 applied and that a different conclusion would give rise to difficulties.

Finally, the OECD Report leaves the whole question open. The Report only mentions that two different approaches could be applied which is not entirely new. It even does not give the reasonings behind each approach. Furthermore, the information that one approach is agreed by the majority and the other approach by a minority is not helpful. Since the Report does not give the arguments, it does not enable practitioners worldwide to follow the approach which seems to be most convincing. Therefore the question arises, why Example 12 above was inserted in the Report.

13. Determination of 'Employer' for the Purposes of Article 15

88. During its discussion on whether partnerships qualify as residents for purposes of tax Conventions, the Committee also examined a related issue arising from the reference to the concept of resident in subparagraph 2(b) of Article 15. Paragraph 2 of Article 15 exempts employment income earned by a resident of a Contracting State in the other State from tax by that other State if a number of conditions apply. One such condition is that the employer must not be a resident of the State in which the employment income is earned. The application of this rule may be problematic when the employer is a partnership.

89. As discussed above, a partnership that is treated as a transparent entity by a Contracting State does not qualify as a resident of that State under Article 4. While it is clear that a partnership that is treated as a transparent entity could qualify as an 'employer' (especially under the domestic law definitions of the term in some countries, e.g., where an employer is defined as a person liable for a wage tax), the application of the condition imposed by subparagraph 2(b) of Article 15 at the level of the partnership regardless of the situation of the partners would render the condition totally meaningless because the partnership cannot possibly qualify as a resident by virtue of its transparent status.

90. The Committee examined this result in the context of Article 15 and in light of the object and purpose of subparagraph 2(b) and (c) of that Article. In its view, the conditions imposed by these subparagraphs aim at avoiding the source taxation of short-term employments to the extent that the employment income is not allowed as a deductible expense in the State of source because the employer is not taxable in that State as he is not resident nor has a permanent establishment therein. These subparagraphs can also be justified by the fact that imposing source deduction requirements with respect to short-term employments in a given State may be considered to constitute an excessive administrative burden where the employer neither resides nor has a permanent establishment in that State.

91. On that basis, the Committee concluded that in order to achieve a meaningful interpretation that would accord with the context and the object of paragraph 2 of Article 15, subparagraph 2(b) should, in the case of partnerships treated as transparent entities, be considered to refer to the partners of such as partnership. Thus, the Committee favours an interpretation where the concepts of 'employer' and 'resident', as found in subparagraph 2(b), are applied at the level of the partners rather than at the level of the partnership. This approach is fully consistent with that put forward in paragraphs 81 and 85 above, under which certain provisions of tax Conventions must be applied at the partners' level

rather than at that of the partnership in order to avoid absurd or unreasonable results.

92. The Committee realised that this interpretation would create difficulties where the partners reside in different States. Such difficulties, however, could be addressed through the mutual agreement procedure by reference, for example, to the State in which the partners who own the majority of the interests in the partnership reside (i.e., the State in which the greatest part of the deduction will be claimed).

The approach to look through the partnership and focus on the partners suggested in the OECD Report seems to be convincing. The arguments put forward are persuasive. However, it is striking that the OECD Report does not contain an example in this respect. The mere academic description of the problem leaves the impression that the situation is as simple. However, in comparison to the first examples, a lot of distinctions could be made. The OECD Report obviously assumes that both the State where the partnership is established and the State where the partners are residents treat the partnership as a transparent entity. But what is the impact on the tax treaty application, if, for example, the State of which one of the partners is a resident treats the partnership as a taxable entity?

However, even the solution suggested in the OECD Report for a situation where both countries apply an approach based on a transparency concept, is weakened in paragraph 92. The Committee 'realized that this interpretation would create difficulties where the partners reside in different States' and suggests therefore that these difficulties 'could be addressed through the mutual agreement procedure'. It is striking that the OECD Report mentions difficulties and ways to avoid these difficulties in this respect, although in the context of other situations such administrative difficulties have to be overcome. Furthermore, it would be interesting to know to what end the suggested mutual agreement procedure could lead. As the OECD Report convincingly suggests to apply a look-through approach, there seems to be no other way that more convincing arguments could be developed through a mutual agreement procedure.

14. Example 13

Partner A makes a loan to partnership P, which has been established in State P where it carries on a business through a permanent establishment. P pays interest to A. State P recognizes loans between partners and partnerships; under its domestic legislation State P allows P a tax deduction for the interest. State R does not recognize loans between partners and partnerships under its domestic law. Both States treat partnerships as transparent entities and apply Article 7 to the income of P, but State P applies Article 11 to the interest payment and State R does not.

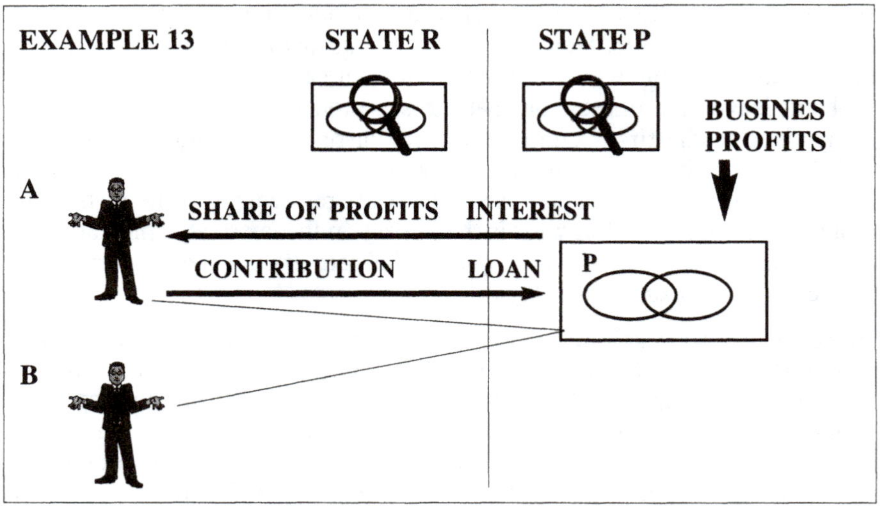

96. In this example, while partner A is clearly entitled to the benefits of the R-P Convention, there is disagreement between State P and R as to which provisions of the Convention are applicable. State P, being the State of source of the income, applies its domestic laws for the purposes of taxing the income of, and from, the partnership. It accordingly determines that partner A receives interest from the partnership and that Article 11 of the Convention applies to restrict to 10 per cent the tax that it can impose on the interest. Under the domestic law of State R, there has been no loan and consequently A has no interest income. State R, however, will consider that the payment from P to A is a distribution of A's share of the business profits of the partnership which has been taxed upon realization under Article 7.
97. The position of State P is in accordance with the provisions of the Convention. Pursuant to paragraph 2 of Article 3, State P has interpreted the word 'debt-claims of every kind', which are found in paragraph 3 of Article 11, in accordance with its domestic law and has therefore con-

cluded that a loan by a partner qualifies as a debt-claim on which interest may be paid. It has applied Article 11 of the Convention accordingly.

98. The consequences of the position taken by State P must, however, be examined in relation to the taxation of Partner A in State R. One must distinguish, in that respect, the cases where State R eliminates double taxation through the exemption method from those where it applies the credit method.

99. Under the domestic law of State R, there is no debt-claim between partner A and the partnership and A therefore does not derive interest from State P. If State R follows that position when considering its obligation to eliminate double taxation under Article 23A, that could lead it to consider that the payment made to partner A is a distribution of the partnership's business profits which is attributable to a permanent establishment situated in State P which constitutes income that must be exempted under paragraph 1 of Article 23A. To the extent that State P would have interpreted the Convention as obliging it to limit its tax to 10 per cent of the gross amount of the payment, the result would be partial non-taxation (it would be total non-taxation if Article 11 of the R-P Convention did not provide for any source taxation of interest).

100. It must be noted that, regardless of the Convention, State R may still be obliged to exempt the income under its domestic tax rules related to the elimination on double taxation as these rules may require that another approach be followed. This, however, would be a problem that could only be solved through an amendment to State R's domestic laws.

101. Under the domestic law of State R, there is no debt-claim between partner A and the partnership and A therefore does not derive interest from State P. Even if State R follows that position when considering its obligation to eliminate double taxation under Article 23B, it should still tax any share of the partnership's income attributed to A so that non-taxation will be avoided.

119. Starting with Example 13 above (the facts of that example appear in subsection (a)), it should be concluded that in that example, the partial non-taxation referred to in paragraph 99 above will be avoided since State R will not be required to exempt what State P considers as interest since it may be said that State P may, under its domestic law, tax that part of the income of the partnership under paragraph 2 of Article 11. State R will therefore apply the credit method in that case, either under paragraph 2 of Article 23A (exemption method) or under paragraph 1 of Article 23B (credit method).

The OECD Report contains a lengthy discussion to solve the qualification conflict described in Example 13 above. The reason why so many arguments are put forward is that a solution that could lead to double non-taxation does not seem satisfactory to the Committee. Therefore, one has to emphasize that the OECD Report does not thoroughly distinguish between arguments relevant for the interpretation of the provisions in question on the one hand and the mere political deliberations of the members of the Committee on the other hand. As already repeatedly pointed out, the prevention of double non-taxation is to date not part of the object and purpose of the OECD Model Tax Convention. Therefore, all arguments based on the idea to prevent double non-taxation may not be taken into account as far as the interpretation of the existing version of the OECD Model Tax Convention is concerned.

Furthermore, the OECD Report tries to solve a problem which it previously created: the OECD Report takes the position that both States are free to qualify the loan according to their domestic law. Although the OECD Report mentions Article 3 paragraph 2 of the OECD Model Tax Convention in this respect, the Committee does not examine if a solution deriving from the 'context' of the treaty could be suggested: such an approach could focus on the fact that both countries do not treat the partnership as a taxable entity and therefore look to the partners. Article 11 paragraph 5 of the OECD Model Tax Convention indicates that interest could be paid from one taxable entity to another taxable entity. Therefore, one arrives at a solution suggesting that the payment between A and the partnership has to be split.[85] As A and B are the partners, to a certain extent A is deemed to pay interest and to a certain extent B is deemed to pay interest, depending on their respective shares as partners. Since the qualification of 'interest' according to the above-mentioned context of the tax treaty requires that the person paying the interest and the person receiving the interest are not identical, one must not assume that A pays interest to himself.[86] Therefore, the income A receives for lending money to the partnership qualifies to a certain extent as 'interest', depending on the share of profits the other partners usually receive.[87] The remaining amount may be treated under Article 7 of the OECD Model Tax Convention. If both States try to arrive at a solution deriving from the context of the tax treaty it is very likely that they come to this result.

However, as the OECD Report does not take that position, the Committee arrives at a solution providing for a partial or even a full double non-taxation, if the exemption method is applied in the State of residence. To avoid this result, the Committee refers to its deliberations on the meaning of the phrase 'in accordance with the provisions of this Convention'.[88] The Committee develops an approach according to which this provision is understood as a

[85] M. Lang, *Finanzierungen*, pp. 97 et seq.

[86] M. Lang, *Finanzierungen*, p. 98.

[87] M. Lang, *Finanzierungen*, p. 98; M. Lang, in Kleineidam (ed.), *FS Lutz Fischer* (1999) p. 725.

[88] OECD, supra note 1, para 104.

reference to the domestic law of the source State. Whenever the source State imposes taxes 'in accordance with the provisions of this Convention', the residence State shall be bound by the decision made by the authorities of the source State.

The OECD Report admits that the residence State is not bound by the source State in any case. According to paragraph 105, part of the general deliberations of the OECD Report in this respect, 'due to differences in the domestic law between the State of source and the State of residence, the former applies, with respect to a particular item of income, provisions of the Convention that are different from those that the State of residence would have applied to the same item of income, the income is still being taxed in accordance with the provisions of the Convention, in this case as interpreted by the State of source'.[89] Therefore, the residence State is not bound by the interpretation favoured in the source State, if pure tax treaty law is at stake. Subsequently, it is decisive if an interpretation of a provision can derive from the 'context' or if—according to Article 3 paragraph 2 of the OECD Model Tax Convention—recourse has to be taken to the domestic law of the source State. It is obvious that the answer to this question can be anything but clear. Even Example 13 above demonstrates this: as shown above, it is possible to arrive at an interpretation derived from the 'context'. Nevertheless, the OECD Report ignores this possibility and takes recourse to domestic law without examining if the 'context' requires another interpretation.

[89] OECD, supra note 1, para 105.

15. Example 14

Partner A, a resident of State R, sells his interest in P to D, a resident of State P, for an amount that exceeds A's adjusted basis in the interest. Under State R's domestic law, State R treats P as a company and would regard the gain as a capital gain of a resident of State R. Under State P's domestic law, State P treats P as fiscally transparent and would regard the gain as attributable to a State P permanent establishment.

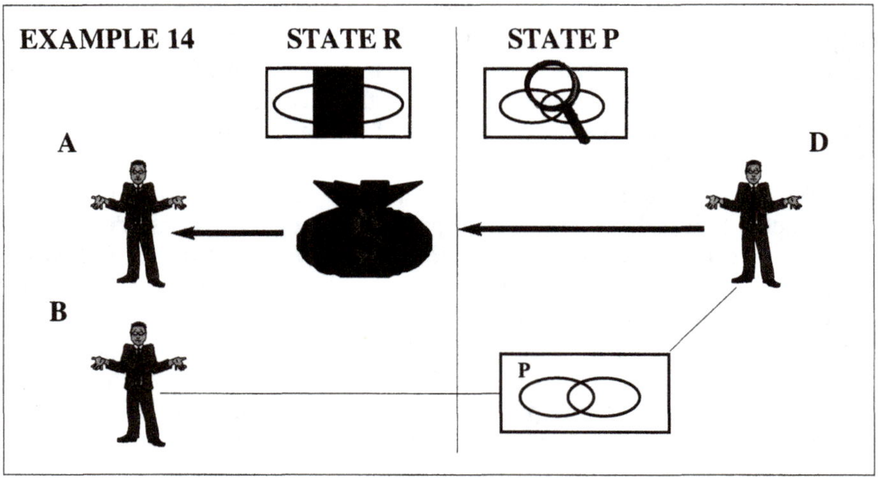

107. In this example, State P therefore considers that the alienation of the interest in the partnership is, for the purposes of its Convention with State R, an alienation by the partner of the underlying assets of the business carried on by the partnership, which may be taxed by State P according to paragraph 1 or 2 of Article 13. State R, as it treats the partnership as a corporate entity, considers that the alienation of the interest in the partnership is akin to the alienation of a share in a company, which could not be taxed by State P by reason of paragraph 4 of Article 13. In such a case, the conflict of qualification results exclusively from the different treatment of partnerships in the domestic laws of the two States and State P must be considered by State R to have taxed the gain from the alienation 'in accordance with the provisions of the Convention' for the purposes of the application of Article 23. State R must therefore grant an exemption or give a credit pursuant to Article 23 of the Model Tax Convention irrespective of the fact that, under its own domestic law, it treats the alienation gain as income from the disposition of shares in a corporate entity and that, if State's P qualification of the income were consistent with that of State R, State R would not have to give relief under Article 23. No double taxation will therefore arise in such a case.

108. This does not mean that the wording of Article 23 requires the State of residence to eliminate double taxation in all cases where the State of source has imposed its tax by applying to an item of income a provision of the Convention that is different from that which the State of residence considers to be applicable. For instance, in the example above, if, for purposes of applying paragraph 2 of Article 13, State P considers that the partnership carried on business through a fixed place of business but State R argues that paragraph 4 applies because the partnership did not have a fixed place of business in State P, there is a legitimate dispute as to whether State P has taxed the income in accordance with the provisions of the Convention. The same may be said if State P, when applying paragraph 2 of Article 13, has interpreted the phrase 'forming part of the business property' so as to include certain assets which would not fall within the meaning of that phrase according to the interpretation given to it by State R. Such conflicts resulting from a different interpretation of facts or a different interpretation of the provisions of the Convention must be distinguished from the conflicts of qualification described in the above paragraph where the divergence is based not on different interpretations of the provisions of the Convention, but on different provisions of domestic law. In the former case, the State of residence can argue that the State of source has not imposed its tax in accordance with the provisions of the Convention, it has applied its tax based on what the State of residence considers to be a wrong interpretation of the facts or a wrong interpretation of the Convention. States should use the provisions of Article 25 (Mutual Agreement Procedure), and in particular paragraph 3 thereof, in order to resolve this type of conflict when the difference in approaches would otherwise result in unrelieved double taxation.

109. In other situations, however, the phrase 'in accordance with the provisions of this Convention, may be taxed' need to be interpreted in relation to possible cases of double non-taxation involving residence States that follow the exemption method. Where the State of source considers that the provisions of the Convention preclude it from taxing an item of income which it would otherwise have taxed, the State of residence should, for purposes of applying paragraph 1 of Article 23A, consider that the item of income may not be taxed by the State of source in accordance with the provisions of the Convention, even though the State of residence would have applied the Convention differently so as to tax that income if it had been the State of source. Thus the State of residence is not required by paragraph 1 to exempt the item of income, a result which is consistent with the basic function of Article 23 which is to eliminate double taxation.

110. This situation may be illustrated by reference to the facts of the above example. A business is carried on through a fixed place of business in

State P by a partnership established in that State and a partner, resident in State R, alienates his interest in that partnership. Changing the facts of the example, however, it is now assumed that State P treats the partnership as a taxable entity whereas State R treats it as fiscally transparent; it is further assumed that State R is an exemption State. State P, as it treats the partnership as a corporate entity, considers that the alienation of the interest in the partnership is akin to the alienation of a share in a company, which it cannot tax by reason of paragraph 4 of Article 13. State R, on the other hand, considers that the alienation of the interest in the partnership should have been taxable by State P as an alienation by the partner of the underlying assets of the business carried on by the partnership to which paragraph 1 or 2 of Article 13 would have been applicable. In determining whether it has the obligation to exempt the income under paragraph 1 of Article 23A, State R should nonetheless consider that, given the way that the provisions of the Convention apply in relation to the domestic law of State P, that State may not tax the income in accordance with the provisions of the Convention; State R is thus under no obligation to exempt the income.

111. Such cases should not be confused with cases where the provisions of a Convention grant, to the source State, the right to tax an item of income but that item of income is not taxed under the domestic law of the State of source. In such cases, the State of residence must still exempt that item of income under the provisions of paragraph 1 of Article 23A (compare paragraph 34 of the Commentary on Article 23).

112. Other cases that need to be distinguished are those where the double non-taxation results from disagreements between the State of residence and the State of source on the interpretation of the provisions of the Convention. In such cases, the State of residence does not agree that, in relation to the domestic law of the State of source, that State is precluded from taxing the item of income. The State of residence is therefore arguing that, to the extent that its interpretation of the Convention is correct, it has to grant exemption. Conversely, the source State is arguing that, if its interpretation of the Convention is the correct one, it cannot tax the income and the residence State should therefore not grant exemption. A similar problem could arise in the case of different interpretations of facts.

113. The Committee decided that the best way of addressing such cases of double non-taxation would be through a provision, to be added to Article 23A, that would provide that the residence State does not have to grant exemption in these cases. Such a provision would deal with cases of double non-taxation resulting from different interpretations of the provisions of the Convention or of the facts. The Committee there-

fore decided that the following paragraph 4 be added to Article 23A of the Model Tax Convention:

> '4. The provisions of paragraph 1 shall not apply to income derived or capital owned by a resident of a Contracting State where the other Contracting State applies the provisions of this Convention to exempt such income or capital from tax or applies the provisions of paragraph 2 of Article 10 or 11 to such income'.

114. This proposed provision would only apply to the extent that the State of source has applied the provisions of the Convention to exempt an item of income or capital or has applied the provisions of paragraph 2 of Articles 10 or 11 to an item of income. The paragraph would therefore not apply where the State of source considers that it may tax an item of income or capital in accordance with the provisions of the Convention but where no tax is actually payable on such income or capital under the provisions of the domestic laws of the State of source. Similarly, where the source and residence States disagree not only with respect to the qualification of the income but also with respect to the amount of such income, paragraph 4 applies only to that part of income that the State of source exempts from tax through the application of the Convention or to which that State applies paragraph 2 of Articles 10 or 11.

115. The preceding comments concern the position of the residence State where the wording of the provisions on elimination of double taxation in the relevant bilateral Convention is similar to that of Article 23 of the Model Tax Convention. Where, however, the wording is different from that used in the Model Tax Convention, the result might also be different.

116. One variation that is often found in bilateral Conventions is to begin the Article on elimination of double taxation with the words '(double taxation shall be avoided as follows: (...)'. Where such wording is used, the conclusions presented in the preceding paragraphs would be reinforced since these words make it clear that the article is intended to apply only where there is double taxation and the obligation imposed on the Contracting States to avoid double taxation will best be satisfied by adopting the approach described in this section.

117. In some Conventions, the Article on elimination of double taxation includes an explicit reference to internal law, e.g., requiring a credit for foreign taxes to be granted subject to the provisions of the domestic law regarding the crediting against domestic law of tax payable in the other State but without affecting the general principle provided in the article. While the effect of these provisions has to be determined on the basis of their precise wording, such wording, which provides that the reference to domestic law should not affect the principle of the treaty article, will

> generally allow the application of the conclusions of the preceding paragraphs. In some Conventions, however, the reference to domestic law is not so limited, provided that any inconsistency between the domestic law and the treaty rules existed at the time of signature of the Convention. To avoid confusion, Contracting States may wish to make clear the extent to which domestic law will control in situations existing at the time of entry into force of the Convention where the application of the domestic provision could be said to be inconsistent with the 'general principle' of achieving double tax relief.

Again, the OECD Report fails to examine if an interpretation from the 'context' of the treaty can be derived. It can easily be shown that such an attempt would have been successful. One must not ignore that the four paragraphs of Article 13 of the OECD Model Tax Convention which refer to various other provisions of the OECD Model Tax Convention, e.g., Article 13 paragraph 1 refers explicitly to Article 6 of the OECD Model Tax Convention, paragraph 2 refers implicitly to Article 7 and Article 14, and paragraph 3 refers implicitly to Article 8 of the OECD Model Tax Convention. Therefore the phrase 'property other than that referred to in paragraphs 1, 2 and 3' must be interpreted by looking at all the other distributive rules in paragraph 1 to 3 neither explicitly nor implicitly referred to. The qualification of the property for the purpose of the various paragraphs of Article 13 depends on the qualification of the income deriving from this property. As far as income deriving from a foreign partnership is concerned, the qualification of this income depends on the tax treatment of this partnership in the other Contracting State. If the other Contracting State treats the partnership as a taxable entity, Article 10 of the OECD Model Tax Convention is applicable, since 'income from ... corporate rights' falls under Article 10 paragraph 3 of the OECD Model Tax Convention, if the income 'is subjected to the same taxation treatment as income from shares by the laws of the State of which the company making the distribution is a resident'. Therefore, gains from the alienation of an interest in a partnership, which is treated as a taxable entity by the State of source, would fall under Article 13 paragraph 4 of the OECD Model Tax Convention. If the other Contracting State, however, does not treat the partnership as a taxable entity, Article 10 cannot be applicable. Instead, one has to assume that the partnership will constitute a permanent establishment for the partners. The profits will fall under Article 7 of the OECD Model Tax Convention. As Article 13 refers to the other distributive rules under which the income deriving from the property falls, this distinction is, in paying attention to the context of the treaty, also relevant for Article 13 of the OECD Model Tax Convention. Therefore, gains from the alienation of an interest in a partnership which is treated as transparent by the State of source fall under Article 13 paragraph 2 of the OECD Model Tax Convention. This interpretation does not derive from the application of Article 3 paragraph 2 of the OECD Model Tax

Convention. No recourse to domestic law is necessary because the 'context' does not 'otherwise require'. On the contrary, in such a situation, it is the context which requires recourse to the domestic treatment in the source State.

Following this approach, there is no need to understand the phrase 'in accordance with the provisions of this Convention' in the manner the OECD Report suggests. There is no qualification conflict which can only be solved by interpreting this phrase in a new manner. Even if one understands the above-mentioned phrase as suggested by the OECD Report, the relevance of the domestic law of the source State does not derive from Article 23. Since the context indicates the interpretation, it is not due to domestic law as referred to in Article 3 paragraph 2 of the OECD Model Tax Convention that the source State's domestic law is relevant. Therefore, neither the phrase 'in accordance with the provisions of this Convention' nor the suggested Article 23 paragraph 4 can be applicable.

16. Example 15

The facts are the same as in Example 13 above except that the treatment of the loan in State P and R is reversed. Partner A makes a loan to partnership P, which has been established in State P where it carries on a business through a permanent establishment. P pays interest to A. State R recognizes loans between partners and partnerships but State P does not. Both States treat partnerships as transparent entities and apply Article 7 to the income of P, but State R considers that Article 11 should apply to the payment made to partner A.

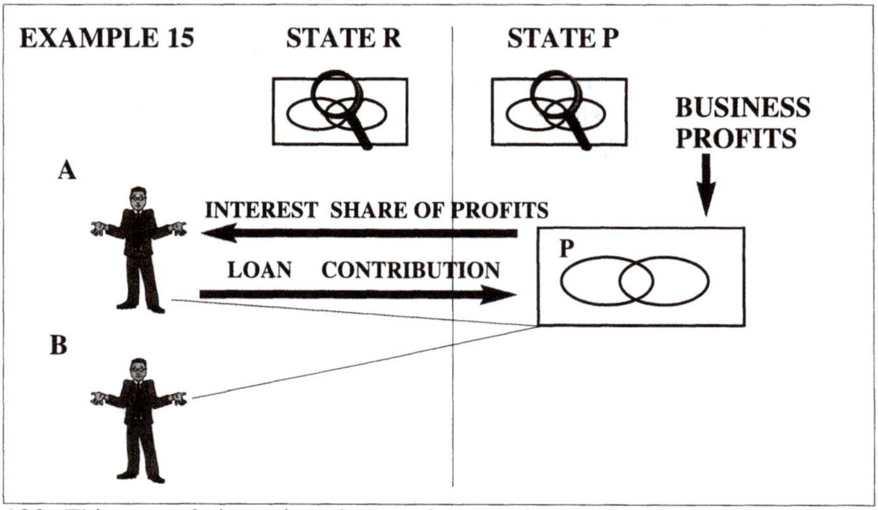

120. This example is a mirror image of the conflict of qualification presented in Example 13 above. State P, as the State of source of the income, determines that the payment is a distribution of partner A's share of the partnership business profits and that Article 7 of the Convention applies to allow it to tax that share without restriction. State R, however, considers that the payment from P to A is a payment of interest subject to the rules of Article 11.

121. Again, the position of State P is in accordance with the provisions of the Convention. Pursuant to paragraph 2 of Article 3, State P has interpreted the words 'debt-claim of every kind', which are found in paragraph 3 of Article 11, in accordance with its domestic law and has concluded that the financial contribution made by partner A did not qualify as a debt-claim for the purposes of determining whether the payment was interest.

122. As Articles 23A and 23B both provide for the credit method to be applied in relation to interest, it may be argued that the consequences of that position for State R will be the same whether that State eliminates double taxation predominantly through the exemption method or

through the credit method. Under the domestic law of State R, there is a debt-claim and partner A derives interest from State P. If State R follows that position when considering its obligation to eliminate double taxation under Articles 23A or 23B, that could lead it to consider that the payment made to partner A is interest that it may tax, subject to giving a credit for any State P tax levied in accordance with paragraph 2 of Article 11. If the Convention does not allow for source taxation of interest, the result of that approach will be double taxation. If the Convention follows Article 11 of the Model Tax Convention, the application of paragraph 2 of Articles 23A or of paragraph 1 of Article 23B under that approach will likely result in some double taxation to the extent that State R may only give credit for the part of the State P tax that it considers to have been imposed in accordance with Article 11, i.e., 10 per cent of the payment of the interest.

123. On the basis of the principles developed in subsection (b), however, that result will be avoided since State R will be obliged either to exempt what it considers to be interest (if it applies the exemption method) or to give a credit for the full amount of tax levied by State P on that item of income (if it applies the credit method). This is because the tax which State P has levied under Article 7 has been levied in accordance with the provisions of Article 7 of the Convention, taking into account the qualification of the income in light of State P's domestic tax law.

The OECD Report correctly points out that Example 15 above is the mirror image of Example 13 above. According to the OECD Report, in the situation described in Article 15 double taxation would arise, unless the approach applied by the OECD Report is followed. As shown when analysing Example 13 above, this assumption is not correct. The OECD Report fails to examine if an interpretation can be derived from the context of the treaty. As already shown, this is possible. Therefore, there is no need to rely on the approach suggested by the OECD Report to avoid double taxation.

17. Example 16

P is a partnership established in State P. Partner B is a resident of State R while partner A is a resident of State P. State P treats the partnership as a taxable entity while State R treats is as a transparent entity. P derives royalty income from State R that is not attributable to a permanent establishment in State R. P has an office in State P and may therefore be considered to have a permanent establishment in State P.

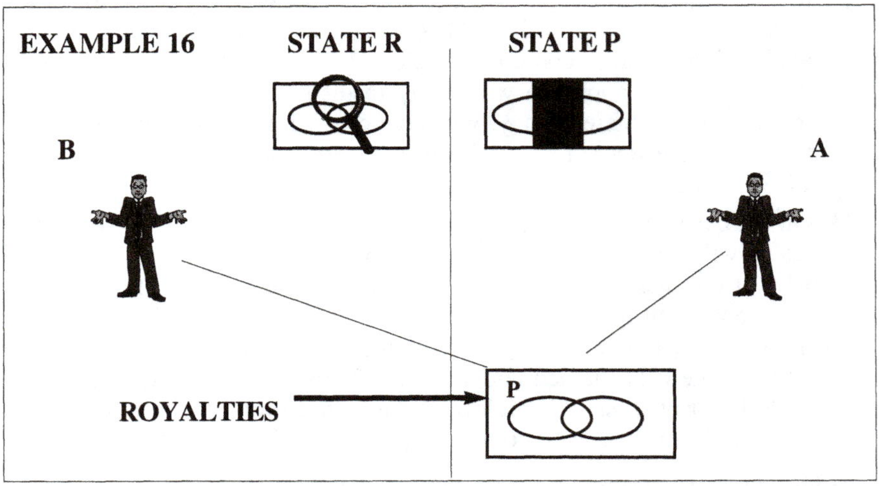

125. In that example, P qualifies as a resident of State P as it is a person 'liable to tax' therein according to the laws of State P. Under Article 12 of the P-R treaty, it is clear that State R cannot tax the partnership on the royalty. State R, however, would like to tax partner B, a resident, on his share of the income of the partnership.

126. Some delegates took the position that the R-P Convention prevents State R from taxing in that situation. On the basis of paragraph 1 of Article 12, which provides that royalties arising in State R and paid to a resident of State P are taxable only in State P if the resident is the beneficial owner thereof, they argued that because the partnership qualifies as a resident of State P, and is the beneficial owner of the royalties, the conditions of the paragraph are met and the royalties may only be taxed in State P. The delegates who adopted that interpretation therefore concluded that unless the case fell under the application of CFC rules or the Convention included a special provision allowing State R to tax its residents in such circumstances (e.g., a specific provision applicable to partnerships or a so-called 'saving clause' such as is found in Conventions concluded by the United States), the Convention would prevent State R from taxing partner B on his share of the royalties.

127. The majority, however, disagreed with that position. When taxing partner B, State R is taxing its own resident on income arising in its territory. Article 12 of the Convention does not affect taxation that is based on residence but only taxation that is based on source. When applying the Convention, State R may indeed consider, based on the principles developed in previous examples, that partner B may be considered to have received payment of his share of the royalties for the purposes of taxation in that State so that the limitation of Article 12 does not apply since that Article is only applicable where royalties arising in one State have been paid to a resident of the other State.

128. The Committee therefore decided that the Commentary on Article 1 be amended by adding the following paragraph thereto:

> 'Where a partnership is treated as a resident of a Contracting State, the provisions of the Convention that restrict the other Contracting State's right to tax the partnership on its income do not apply to restrict that other State's right to tax the partners who are its own residents on their share of the income of the partnership. Some States may wish to include in their Conventions a provision that expressly confirms a Contracting State's right to tax resident partners on their share of the income of a partnership that is treated as a resident of the other State'.

129. Since State R's right to tax partner B on his share of the income of the partnership derives from the partner's residence in that State, it follows that State R must also give the benefits of Article 23 to partner B. The fact that the partnership has a permanent establishment in State P is not relevant in that respect since, as discussed in subsection (b), the tax levied by State P will still have been levied in accordance with the provisions of the Convention since State P is allowed to tax partnership P as its resident. The application of Article 23 by State R may, however, raise some difficulties because State P will levy its tax on the partnership rather than on the partners and because that tax may be levied both when the income is realized and when it is distributed (i.e., through a withholding tax on the distribution which State P may treat as a dividend). These difficulties are examined below in relation to Example 18 below.

It is surprising that rather than the majority only some delegates stuck to the principles developed by the Committee when analyzing the previous examples. If one follows the approach that the tax treatment in the Contracting State, where the recipient of the income is a resident, is relevant for the entitlement to the treaty benefits, it is clear that one has to accept that the partnership is treated as a taxable entity in State P and therefore, according to the above developed principles, entitled to the benefits of the tax treaty between R and P. However, the minority of the Committee thinks that domestic

Controlled Foreign Company (CFC) rules can lead to the denial of treaty benefits, a position which is very questionable and expressed without giving any reasons why domestic law should prevail over tax treaty provisions.

However, as the principles previously developed by the Committee are not convincing, one might apply another approach. According to State R, the source State of the royalties, the royalty income is allocated to A and B. As B is a resident of State R, B may claim benefits provided by tax treaties concluded by State R. However, Article 12 of the OECD Model Tax Convention is not applicable for B, as the royalties did not arise in another Contracting State. Therefore Article 7 of the OECD Model Tax Convention seems to be applicable. However, as State P treats P as a taxable entity, Article 10 of the OECD Model Tax Convention is applicable. This provision prevails over Article 7 of the OECD Model Tax Convention. According to Article 10 of the OECD Model Tax Convention, State R may tax the income. Therefore, even the source taxation of the royalties is covered by the treaty, as the whole income of the partnership including the royalties may be taxed in R, as far as the share of B is concerned.

As far as the share of A is concerned, the royalties are allocated to A to a certain extent, according to the domestic law of State R. As A is a resident of State P, Article 12 of the OECD Model Tax Convention is applicable. Article 12 of the OECD Model Tax Convention prevails over Article 7 of the OECD Model Tax Convention. Therefore, Article 10 of the OECD Model Tax Convention is not applicable either: although the partnership is a resident of one State, namely State P, it is a resident of the same State of which A is a resident. As the application of Article 10 of the OECD Model Tax Convention requires the corporate entity to be a resident of the other State, the preconditions for the application of Article 10 are not fulfilled, as far as A is concerned.

Summing up, the principles developed by the Committee lead to results which cannot be supported even by its own majority. Therefore, it is suggested to follow more convincing principles whose application lead to results the majority of the Committee obviously could support.

18. Example 17

P is a partnership established in State P. A and B are P's partners who reside in State R. State P treats P as a taxable entity while State R treats it as a transparent entity. P derives royalty income from State P that is not attributable to a permanent establishment in that State.

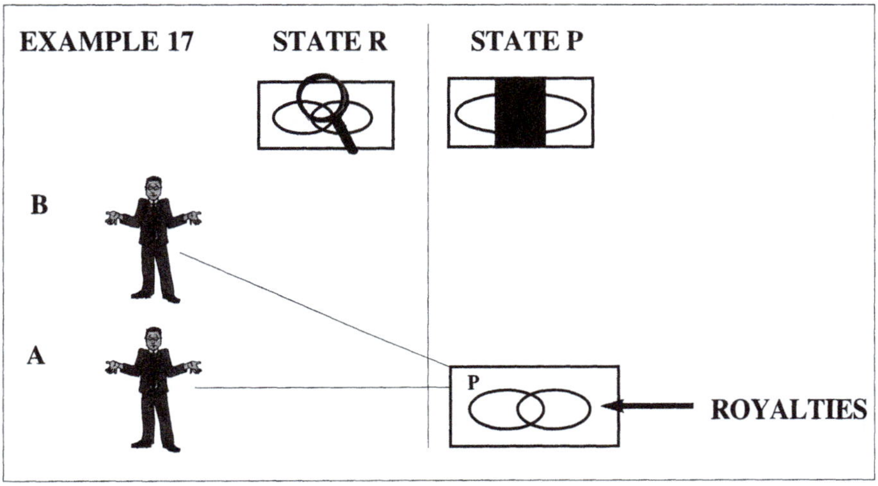

130. This example addresses a factual situation similar to that described in the preceding example but from the perspective of the State of residence of the partnership, i.e., State P. In this example, State P would, under its domestic law, impose tax on the royalties in the hands of the partnership. From its perspective, P is a resident taxpayer and as such liable to tax on its income arising in State P. Thus, Article 12 of the Convention would not apply since the royalties arise in State P and are paid to a resident of State P. However, because State R allocates the income to partners A and B, they are also liable to tax on the royalties in State R as residents. There would thus be double taxation on the same item of income because of the differing allocation rules in this situation.

131. The majority was of the view that, despite the general principles discussed in Section II.5 which would require the source State to take into consideration the treatment of the income in the State of the residence of the partners, in this situation State P would not be limited in its taxing rights by the P-R Convention. In its view, the situation involves a purely domestic matter from the perspective of State P; it is simply taxing the domestic source income of a resident taxpayer and nothing in the Convention can limit that right. The fact that double taxation results because of the differing income allocations of State R and P is not a reason to limit its right to tax its residents.

132. Some delegates, however, would continue to follow the principle that State P, in applying the Convention, should take into account the fact that, under the allocation of income rules in State R, the income would be liable to tax in the hands of A and B. Their position would be that State P is obliged to relieve the potential resulting double taxation by applying Article 12 to exempt the income in the hands of the partners, thus leaving the exclusive taxing right with State R.

133. Where P continues to tax income in the hands of P, the possible application of Article 23 is discussed in Section III.1.

Again, the majority of the Committee is willing to accept a result which is in contradiction to the previously developed principles, obviously, because one of the Contracting States would have to give up his taxing right. However, the majority fails to realize that even considering the recipient of the income, although A and B are entitled to the treaty benefits, Article 12 of the OECD Model Tax Convention is not applicable. Article 12 paragraph 3 of the OECD Model Tax Convention provides for an exception of Article 12 of the OECD Model Tax Convention if the beneficial owner 'carries on business in the other Contracting State in which the royalties arise, through a permanent establishment situated therein, ... and the right or property in respect of which the royalties are paid is effectively connected with such permanent establishment'. According to the last sentence of Article 12 paragraph 3 of the OECD Model Tax Convention the provisions of Article 7 shall apply in such case. If the partnership constitutes a permanent establishment in State P, State P has the taxing rights under Article 7 of the OECD Model Tax Convention. However, as State P treats the partnership as a taxable entity, income deriving from this partnership falls under Article 10 of the OECD Model Tax Convention. Article 10 of the OECD Model Tax Convention prevails over Article 7 of the OECD Model Tax Convention. According to Article 10 of the OECD Model Tax Convention the residence State may tax. Therefore the income of the partnership including the royalties may be taxed in State R.

As P is a taxable entity of its own, according to the domestic law of State P, State P may also levy taxes. According to Article 7 of the OECD Model Tax Convention, State P may tax if the royalties are part of business profits.

In this situation, double taxation cannot be avoided: State P taxes the income of the partnership including the royalties at the level of the partnership. Therefore, State R is not obliged to credit the tax levied in State P against the individual income tax of the partners A and B.[90]

---

[90] Leitner and Gahleitner, 'Zur Behandlung von Personengesellschaften im Abkommensrecht' (1998) *SWI*, p. 568 (p. 572).

19. Example 18

In Year 1, P, which is established and has a permanent establishment in State P, earns profits of 1 million. In year 2, P distributes to A, a resident of State R, his share in the profits earned in year 1 (300,000). Under State P's domestic law, P is a company, and the profits would be taxed in year 1 at 40 per cent (400,000). In year 2, a further withholding tax (30,000) on the distribution to A would be imposed (by treating it as a dividend). Under State R's domestic law, P is fiscally transparent, and State R would tax A in year 1 on A's share in P's profits (500,000). State R would treat the distribution in year 2 as having no tax effect.

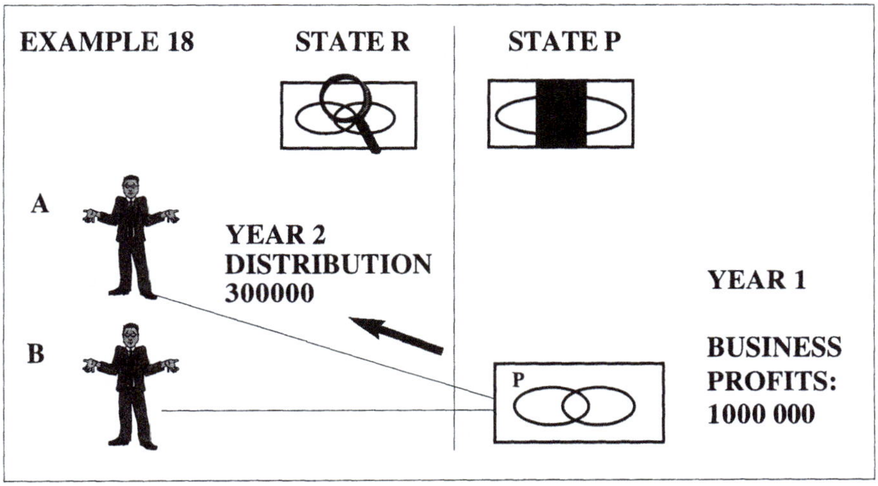

134. In this example, the conflict in income allocation that results from the different treatment of partnerships in States P and R raises the following various difficulties with respect to the elimination of double taxation by State R:
    - the fact that State P taxes two different events (the earning of the profits and their distribution) while State R only takes one event (the earning of the profits);
    - the timing mismatch that results from the fact that State P taxes the distribution in year 2 but State R imposes its tax in year 1;
    - the fact that the State P tax, which is levied when the profits are earned, is paid by the partnership while the State R tax is levied on the partners.

135. The first difficulty relates to whether State R should provide credit for the tax levied by State P upon the distribution. This is an issue that equally concerns States applying the exemption method and States

applying the credit method. If State R applies the exemption method, it must refrain from taxing the partnership's business profits derived from State P in year 1 (it is, of course, entitled to take the excluded income into account in determining the rate of tax on A's remaining income pursuant to paragraph 3 of Article 23A); if it is a credit State, it must give credit for the State P's tax levied on these profits in year 1. In both cases, however, the Convention theoretically requires that it should provide a credit for State P's tax levied on the distribution against its tax on such a distribution (paragraph 2 of Article 23A and paragraph 1 of Article 23B).

136. Since, however, State R does not tax the distribution, there is no tax levied by State R against which to credit State P's tax levied upon the distribution. While the Convention would allow State R to tax the profit distribution made in year 2, such taxation would be inconsistent with State R's treatment of partnership and is therefore not allowed by its domestic law. Under that law, the income may be taxed (subject to any relief from double taxation) only in the year it was earned, i.e., year 1. The matter in which taxation rights allowed by a treaty are exercised is, of course, a matter of domestic law.

137. A clear distinction must be made between the generation of profits and the distribution of those profits. State R, if it is an exemption State, has to exempt from tax the generation of profits in year 1 and therefore is not permitted under the Convention to tax the profits when earned on the basis that Article 10 would allow them to be taxed when distributed. Similarly, however, State R (if it is a credit State) should not be expected to credit the tax levied by State P upon distribution against its own tax levied upon generation.

138. Once it is agreed that State R does not have to levy tax on the distribution, the second difficulty, the timing mismatch, is no longer relevant. While timing mismatches frequently create problems for foreign tax credit purposes which leads States to adopt rules allowing for the carry-back or carry-forward of foreign tax credits, the issue does not arise in this example since there is no double taxation of the distribution.

139. The third difficulty concerns only States that apply the credit method and relates to the fact that both States impose tax upon the same income, but on different taxpayers. The issue is therefore whether State R, which taxes partner A on his share in the partnership profits, is obliged, under the Convention, to give credit for the source tax that is levied in State P on partnership P, which State P treats as a separate taxable entity. The answer to that question must be affirmative. To the extent that State R flows-through the income of the partnership to the partners for the purpose of taxing them, it should be consistent and flow-through the tax paid by the partnership for the purposes of eliminating

double taxation arising from its taxation of the partners. In other words, if the corporate status given to the partnership by State P is ignored for purposes of taxing the share in the profits, it should likewise be ignored for purposes of giving access to the foreign tax credit.

Obviously the Committee assumes that the business profits fall under Article 7 of the OECD Model Tax Convention. The members of the Committee assume that the partnership constitutes a permanent establishment for the partners. As a consequence, State P has the taxing rights. State R has either to exempt the foreign income or to credit the foreign tax. However, this assumption can be challenged: one has to examine if Article 10 of the OECD Model Tax Convention can be applied. The Committee answers this question affirmatively as far as the distributions are concerned. However, is there really a good argument why the business profits should not fall under Article 10 of the OECD Model Tax Convention too? Article 10 of the OECD Model Tax Convention covers, according to its paragraph 3, 'income from ... corporate rights'. Since the partnership is treated as a taxable entity in State P and Article 10 paragraph 3 of the OECD Model Tax Convention refers to the tax treatment in State P for that qualification, all income generated by the corporate rights fall under Article 10 of the OECD Model Tax Convention. However, this is also true for the profits generated by the partnership. Therefore Article 10 of the OECD Model Tax Convention is applicable.[91] Nevertheless, Article 7 of the OECD Model Tax Convention is applicable as well. However, in such a situation Article 10 of the OECD Model Tax Convention has predominance over Article 7 of the OECD Model Tax Convention. According to Article 10 of the OECD Model Tax Convention, State R has the taxing rights. It is up to State R to impose taxes in the year the profits are generated or in the year they are distributed.

In case State P levies a withholding tax on the distribution, the Committee correctly points out that the reductions for dividends have to be applied. Furthermore, the consequence of the above argued opinion is that State R has to credit the withholding tax levied in State P. It is evident that the timing mismatch could cause practical problems. However, the tax treaty obligations force State R to reopen the assessment and credit State P's withholding tax.[92]

Although in this author's opinion State R has to apply Article 10 of the OECD Model Tax Convention, the Committee correctly points out that State P may tax the profits generated by the partnership: as State P treats the partnership as a taxable entity, it is entitled to State P's treaty benefits. According to the treaties P has concluded with third States, the partnership receives profits falling under Article 7 of the OECD Model Tax Convention.

[91] M. Lang, in Kleineidam (ed.), *FS Lutz Fischer* (1999) p. 721.

[92] Schuch, 'Der Anrechnungshöchstbetrag' in Gassner, M. Lang and Lechner (eds), *Die Methoden zur Vermeidung der Doppelbesteuerung* (1995) p. 11 (p. 48).

As State P levies taxes on the level of the partnership and State R on the level of the partners, one might assume that the tax levied in State P cannot be credited against the tax levied in State R. Even Article 10 of the OECD Model Tax Convention does not grant an indirect tax credit. Surprisingly, the Committee, however, supports such a tax credit.[93] Certainly it could be seen unsatisfactory if relief from double taxation is not provided by a tax treaty. On the other hand, if the partnership had been treated as a taxable entity in both countries, it would have been clear that both the profits generated by the partnership and the distribution are taxed. This is exactly how corporations are taxed. Therefore, there is no systematic argument to ignore the tax treaty principles in such a situation.

The opinion taken by the Committee will also be incoporated in the Commentary. It has already been pointed out that this can only be of relevance for the interpretation of bilateral tax treaties concluded from now on. However, it is not entirely clear that the opinion contained in the Commentary will prevail: it is still true that systematic arguments lead to another result. Therefore the interpretation of the new bilateral treaties will depend on the weight one gives to the Commentary.

---

[93] OECD, supra note 1, para 139.

V. Conclusion

The OECD Report is remarkable: the tax treatment of partnerships has never been dealt with that extensively before. The Report will provoke many discussions among academics and practitioners worldwide. The findings of the Report will be examined by many other scholars very thoroughly. Research work will benefit from this Report, since a lot of statements may be challenged. Consequently, practitioners will also benefit, as an even stronger in-depth treatment will be given to many practical problems.

However, it is a pity that the OECD Report was published without seeking the advice of academics and practitioners. Even this first analysis shows that many not so convincing conclusions could have been easily avoided and many parts of the Report would have been improved if experts from outside had been given the opportunity to discuss the preliminary conclusions drawn by the Committee. For the future, the OECD should learn from this experience and distribute drafts of Reports before publishing the official version.

www.ingramcontent.com/pod-product-compliance
Lightning Source LLC
Chambersburg PA
CBHW071355230926
51846CB00002B/569
9789041197917